W9-CIA-278

CREATION
of the
MODERN MIDDLE EAST

Israel

CREATION

of the

MODERN MIDDLE EAST

Israel

Second Edition

Louise Chipley Slavicek | Series Editor: Arthur Goldschmidt Jr.

CHELSEA HOUSE
PUBLISHERS
An imprint of Infobase Publishing

Israel, Second Edition

Copyright © 2009 by Infobase Publishing

All rights reserved. No part of this book may be reproduced or utilized in any form or by any means, electronic or mechanical, including photocopying, recording, or by any information storage or retrieval systems, without permission in writing from the publisher. For information contact:

Chelsea House
An imprint of Infobase Publishing
132 West 31st Street
New York NY 10001

Library of Congress Cataloging-in-Publication Data
Slavicek, Louise Chipley, 1956-
  Israel / Louise Chipley Slavicek. — 2nd ed.
    p. cm. — (Creation of the modern Middle East)
  Includes bibliographical references and index.
  ISBN 978-0-7910-9775-5 (hardcover)
  1. Israel—History—Juvenile literature. 2. Jewish-Arab relations—History—
1917-1948—Juvenile literature. 3. Arab-Israeli conflict—Juvenile literature.
I. Title. II. Series.
  DS126.5.S57 2008
  956.9405⊢—dc22   2008016914

Chelsea House books are available at special discounts when purchased in bulk quantities for businesses, associations, institutions, or sales promotions. Please call our Special Sales Department in New York at (212) 967-8800 or (800) 322-8755.

You can find Chelsea House on the World Wide Web at
http://www.chelseahouse.com

Series design by Annie O'Donnell
Cover design by Jooyoung An

Printed in the United States of America

Bang EJB 10 9 8 7 6 5 4 3 2 1

This book is printed on acid-free paper.

All links and Web addresses were checked and verified to be correct at the time of publication. Because of the dynamic nature of the Web, some addresses and links may have changed since publication and may no longer be valid.

Contents

The Birth of
Modern Israel

On a sultry Friday afternoon in May 1948, several hundred men and women gathered in the spacious main hall of the Tel Aviv Art Museum. They had come together to witness a birth—the birth of the nation of Israel. The historic ceremony opened with the somber strains of the anthem "HaTikvah" (Hebrew for "The Hope"), which expresses the deep longing of the Jewish people to return to their historic birthplace of Zion, or Israel:

> *As long as deep in the heart,*
> *The soul of a Jew yearns,*
> *And toward the East*
> *An eye looks to Zion,*
> *Our hope is not yet lost,*
> *The hope of two thousand years,*
> *To be a free people in our land,*
> *The land of Zion and Jerusalem.*
> *To be a free people in our land,*
> *The land of Zion and Jerusalem.*

After the singing of the anthem, 62-year-old David Ben-Gurion, soon to be Israel's first prime minister, began to read aloud the 979 Hebrew words that make up the nation's Proclamation of Independence. Behind the white-haired Ben-Gurion hung the new Israeli flag, at its center a six-pointed blue star composed

An ardent and tireless campaigner for Israel, David Ben-Gurion had worked for years to establish a free Jewish state. His experiences growing up in Poland and living in Ottoman- and British-controlled Palestine fueled his dedication to the Jewish movement and the creation of Israel.

of two triangles—the traditional Jewish symbol known as the Star of David.

In their homes, workplaces, schools, and on the streets of cities and towns throughout the tiny country, thousands of Jewish men, women, and children heard the Proclamation's stirring words broadcast live over radio stations and public address systems. They listened raptly as Ben-Gurion recounted the Jews' ancient bond with Israel, a land they believed God had promised to their Hebrew ancestors during biblical times.

Nearly 2,000 years ago, Ben-Gurion reminded his audience, the Jews had been driven out of their Promised Land by Roman conquerors and dispersed throughout the world. Yet, he avowed, the scattered Jews had "remained faithful" to their ancestral homeland over the millennia. All too often persecuted in the countries where they settled, the exiles never ceased "to hope and pray for their return and the restoration of their national freedom," proclaimed Ben-Gurion, who, like most of his listeners that afternoon, had been born far from the Promised Land, in Eastern Europe.

Right up until the last few decades, a return to Eretz Yisrael (Hebrew for the "land of Israel") had seemed unattainable to most Jews, no more than a fantasy. Then, in the final years of the nineteenth century, Ben-Gurion recalled, a movement called Zionism had appeared in Europe, reviving hopes for a Jewish homeland. Dedicated to settling Jews in Palestine, as the territory that comprised the ancient Kingdom of Israel had been known since Roman days, Zionists viewed the creation of an independent Jewish state as a matter of survival at a time when anti-Semitism (hatred of Jews) was on the rise throughout Europe. Now, three years after World War II, the nightmare of the Holocaust—the massacre by Nazi Germany of 6 million European Jews during the war—had added greater urgency than ever to the Zionists' argument for the "reestablishment of the Jewish State," Ben-Gurion declared.

Moments later, Ben-Gurion solemnly proclaimed the founding of "Medinath Yisrael," (the State of Israel). With these words, Ben-Gurion's Jewish listeners in the Tel Aviv Art Museum and thousands of others all over the country who had strained to hear the historic announcement over crackling radios and loudspeakers, hugged and clapped and cheered wildly.

As it turned out, there would be precious little time for rejoicing. For even as jubilant crowds danced the traditional Jewish circle dance, or hora, of celebration in the streets of Tel Aviv and Jerusalem, troops and tanks were gathering on the frontiers of their new nation, determined to crush it at its birth. Ben-Gurion, who understood only too clearly the dangers facing Israel, wrote in his diary that evening: "The country went wild with joy. But . . . I refrained from rejoicing. The State was established. Our fate now rests in the hands of the defense forces."

By the following morning of May 15, 1948, Israel was under attack by the armed forces of five of its Arab neighbors: Egypt, Transjordan (present-day Jordan), Syria, Lebanon, and Iraq. Unwilling to recognize the right of the State of Israel to exist in a territory already inhabited by hundreds of thousands of Arab and overwhelmingly Muslim Palestinians, they had joined forces to win back the land of Palestine from a people whose ideas and culture were alien to them—a people they viewed as intruders.

A DISPUTED LAND

Ever since Muslim armies burst out of the Arabian Peninsula to spread their new faith of Islam to the world in the seventh century, most of the population of Palestine and the Middle East had been Arabic in language and Islamic in religion. From the very beginning of Zionist immigration to Palestine in the late 1800s, many Arab Palestinians strongly opposed Jewish settlement in the territory, then a Turkish dependency, fearing that the newcomers would come to replace their own people and way of life in the colony.

With the defeat of the Turkish Ottoman Empire in World War I (1914–1918), Palestine fell under British administration. Conflict between Zionists and Arabs escalated during British rule in the face of a massive wave of Jewish immigration to Palestine from Europe during the 1920s and 1930s. Following World War II (1939–1945), Great Britain decided to pull out of Palestine, handing over the dilemma of how to solve the bitter Arab-Jewish dispute over the region to the international peace-keeping organization, the United Nations (UN). After extensive debate, in 1947 the United Nations General Assembly passed a resolution recommending the partition (division) of Palestine into two independent states, one Jewish and one Arab.

Although it was embraced by most Jews, Arab Palestinians and their supporters throughout the Arab world denounced the UN plan, refusing to consider any proposal that would create a Jewish state in Palestine. Within six months of the controversial resolution, the Jews, asserting that international opinion as represented by the UN proposal was behind them, proclaimed the establishment of the State of Israel in the territories assigned to them by the partition plan.

THE CONTINUING CHALLENGE

As it turned out, the Israeli proclamation of statehood in May 1948 and the eight-month-long Arab-Israeli War that erupted the very next day were destined to be only the opening acts of a drama that is still unfolding today. Over the next half century, the young Israeli state would engage in four more major wars with its Arab neighbors in the Middle East and an ongoing and often violent dispute with the Palestinians, who, in the opening years of the twenty-first century, still lack a country of their own. In addition to the daunting challenge of ensuring national security in a hostile environment, Israel has faced enormous economic and social pressures as it has absorbed wave after wave of Jewish immigrants from a myriad of different countries and cultures.

Yet, in spite of the overwhelming internal and external challenges that have confronted Israel since its birth, the tiny nation has managed to survive, and even to prosper. In the 60 years since David Ben-Gurion announced the establishment of Medinath Yisrael, Israel has seen its population rise from just over half a million to nearly 6.8 million, built a dynamic

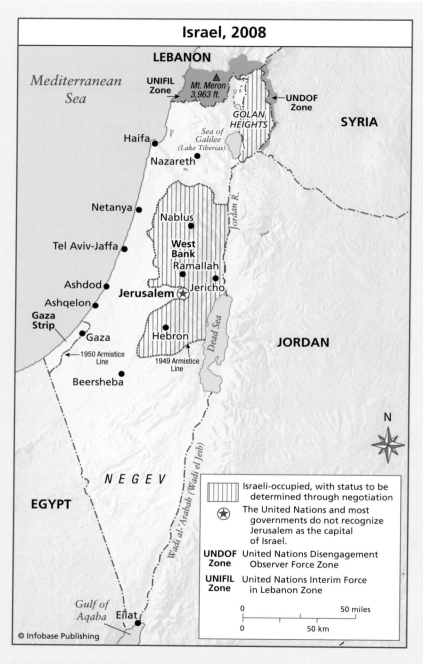

Israel, 2008

LEBANON

Mediterranean Sea

UNIFIL Zone

▲ Mt. Meron 3,963 ft.

← UNDOF Zone

GOLAN HEIGHTS

SYRIA

Haifa

Sea of Galilee (Lake Tiberias)

Nazareth

Jordan R.

Netanya

Nablus

Tel Aviv-Jaffa

West Bank

Ramallah

Ashdod

Jericho

Jerusalem ✪

Ashqelon

Gaza Strip

Gaza

Hebron

Dead Sea

JORDAN

← 1950 Armistice Line

1949 Armistice Line

Beersheba

N

N E G E V

EGYPT

Wadi al-'Arabah (Wadi el Jeib)

	Israeli-occupied, with status to be determined through negotiation
✪	The United Nations and most governments do not recognize Jerusalem as the capital of Israel.
UNDOF Zone	United Nations Disengagement Observer Force Zone
UNIFIL Zone	United Nations Interim Force in Lebanon Zone

0   50 miles

0   50 km

Gulf of Aqaba Eilat

© Infobase Publishing

A little smaller than New Jersey, Israel is the only Jewish state in the world. Jews make up just over 75 percent of Israel's current population of approximately 7 million, while Muslims of Arab descent make up most of the remaining 25 percent.

economy and widely respected educational system, and maintained a lively democracy. During the last decade of the twentieth century, it also appeared as though Israel was well on its way to accomplishing what would arguably be its greatest achievement of all: a peaceful resolution to the nation's long-standing and acrimonious dispute with the Palestinians. Unfortunately, renewed violence between Palestinians and Israelis has gravely threatened the fledgling peace process. It can only be hoped that a productive Palestinian-Israeli dialogue will be resumed during the years ahead, and Israel, which has known almost continuous warfare ever since its establishment, will finally enter a new era of peace.

2

A Promised Land: An Ancient Bond Endures

When the Zionist pioneers began emigrating to Palestine at the end of the nineteenth century, they came to a land with a complicated and troubled past, one whose strategic position at the crossroads of three continents—Asia, Europe, and Africa—had caused it to be invaded and conquered time and again. Yet, although Palestine had been ruled by other peoples throughout much of its long history, the Zionists viewed the sliver of land on the Mediterranean's eastern shore as the eternal Jewish homeland, a land to which Jews had been spiritually and historically linked since the time immortal.

THE JEWS AND THEIR PROMISED LAND

The Jews' bond with Palestine began in about 1800 B.C. when their ancestors, the Hebrews, migrated westward from Mesopotamia to the strip of land bordering the Mediterranean, then called Canaan. Most of what is known about the ancient Hebrews and Canaan comes from the Torah (the first five books of the Old Testament to Christians). According to the Torah, the patriarch Abraham led the Hebrews into Canaan after God promised the land to him and his descendants in return for their devotion and obedience.

After famine struck Canaan, the Hebrews, now generally called the Israelites after Abraham's grandson Israel, fled to Egypt. They stayed in Egypt for some four centuries, much of that time as slaves. In about 1200 B.C., a new leader, Moses, brought the Israelites out of bondage and back toward Canaan.

According to the Torah, Moses led his people as far as the Sinai Desert where God gave him the Ten Commandments, the fundamental religious and moral obligations of the Israelites toward their creator and their fellow humans. God also renewed the covenant (agreement) He had made with Abraham regarding Canaan, promising His "chosen people" eternal ownership of the land if they obeyed his commandments. The first and most important of the commandments God issued to Moses is: "I am the Lord your God. . . . You shall have no other gods before me." The Israelites' monotheism—their belief in a single, all-powerful god—set them apart from the other peoples of the ancient Middle East, who worshipped many gods. Judaism is the name that was eventually given to the unique religion and culture that evolved from the Israelites' monotheistic teachings.

After 40 years in the Sinai Desert, the Israelites finally reentered Canaan, conquering or assimilating most of the other peoples in the region during the next century. In the late eleventh century B.C., they chose the farmer and warrior Saul as their first king. His successor, David, founded the city of Jerusalem on Mount Zion as the Kingdom of Israel's religious and political center and expanded his domain until it reached from the coast of the Mediterranean north into present-day Syria and south to the Red Sea. Israel continued to grow and prosper under the rule of David's son Solomon, who constructed a magnificent temple for the worship of God in Jerusalem.

The golden age of prosperity and power that Israel enjoyed under its three great kings—Saul, David, and Solomon—was destined to be short-lived, however. Following Solomon's death, the kingdom was racked by political strife. In 928 B.C., it split in two, with the northern portion retaining the name of Israel and the southern taking the name Judah. Within two centuries of the partition, the Promised Land would be overrun by the first of a series of conquerors.

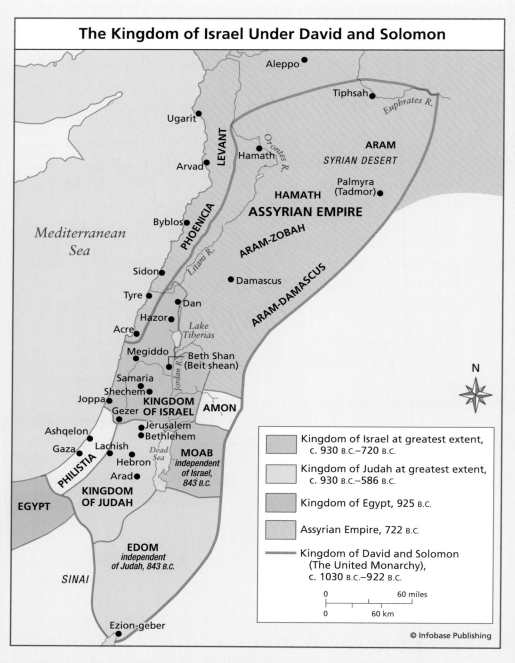

The Kingdom of Israel Under David and Solomon

Aleppo

Tiphsah

Euphrates R.

Ugarit

LEVANT

Orontes R.

Hamath

ARAM

SYRIAN DESERT

Arvad

Palmyra
(Tadmor)

HAMATH

ASSYRIAN EMPIRE

Byblos

PHOENICIA

Litani R.

ARAM-ZOBAH

*Mediterranean
Sea*

Damascus

Sidon

ARAM-DAMASCUS

Tyre

Dan

Hazor

*Lake
Tiberias*

Acre

Megiddo

Beth Shan
(Beit shean)

Jordan R.

Samaria

Shechem

Joppa

**KINGDOM
OF ISRAEL**

AMON

Gezer

Ashqelon

Jerusalem

Bethlehem

Gaza

Lachish

*Dead
Sea*

MOAB
*independent
of Israel,
843 B.C.*

Hebron

Arad

**KINGDOM
OF JUDAH**

EGYPT

EDOM
*independent
of Judah, 843 B.C.*

SINAI

Ezion-geber

N

	Kingdom of Israel at greatest extent, c. 930 B.C.–720 B.C.
	Kingdom of Judah at greatest extent, c. 930 B.C.–586 B.C.
	Kingdom of Egypt, 925 B.C.
	Assyrian Empire, 722 B.C.
	Kingdom of David and Solomon (The United Monarchy), c. 1030 B.C.–922 B.C.

0   60 miles

0   60 km

© Infobase Publishing

Two of the greatest Jewish kings, David and Solomon, encouraged economic
stability and expanded the borders of the kingdom during their reigns. This map
shows the ancient lands that once belonged to the Kingdom of Israel.

A SUCCESSION OF CONQUERORS

During the early eighth century B.C., the Jews entered a long period of virtually unremitting tumult. In 722 B.C., the northern kingdom of Israel disappeared forever when it was overrun and its inhabitants scattered into oblivion by the Assyrians. In 586 B.C., Judah fell to another Middle Eastern superpower—Babylonia. After demolishing the Temple at Jerusalem, the Babylonians marched most of Judah's population in chains to their capital in present-day Iraq. In 539 B.C., the Jewish captives got their chance to go home when Babylonia fell to the Persians (ancestors of the Iranians). Anxious to ensure the support of the many diverse groups living within his empire, the Persian king allowed the Jews to rebuild their devastated kingdom, including the Temple at Jerusalem.

Within two centuries of their triumphant return home, however, the people of Judah confronted a new conqueror: Alexander the Great of Macedon, who crushed the vast Persian Empire in 332 B.C. Following Alexander's death, Judah eventually fell under the control of the Seleucids, a ruling group descended from one of his generals. In 167 B.C., the Seleucid king tried to force all of his subjects to worship the Greek gods. Convinced the survival of their religion was at stake, the Jews revolted under the leadership of Judah the Maccabee. After a long struggle, the rebels expelled the Seleucids, and in 142 B.C. established what was destined to be the last independent Jewish nation until the founding of the State of Israel in 1948.

ROMAN RULE

For nearly a century, Judah remained independent. Then in 63 B.C., the tiny kingdom was overwhelmed by the greatest military power the Mediterranean world had ever seen—the Roman Empire. For the next 500 years, Judah—or Judea as it was now known—would be a Roman colony. It was during the sixth decade of Roman rule that Jesus Christ was born in the province of Judea.

After Jesus's crucifixion in about A.D. 29 by Roman officials who suspected him of trying to incite a rebellion among the Jews, Judea was ruled by a series of especially harsh governors. In 66, the Jews rose up against their brutal overlords, seizing Jerusalem. The rebels were no match for the Romans, however, and within a few years imperial forces had recaptured Jerusalem and destroyed the Jews' holiest shrine, the Temple. Starting in 132, the Jews made one last desperate bid for freedom, but by 135 the Romans had crushed this revolt as well.

Determined to rid themselves of the rebellious Jews, the Romans exiled virtually the entire Jewish population of Judea after the 132–135 revolt, selling hundreds of thousands of men, women, and children into slavery throughout their far-flung empire. To erase all memory of the bond between the Jews and their Promised Land, Judea was officially renamed Palestine. The Romans then imported non-Jews from elsewhere in the Middle East to re-people the land.

Although the vast majority of Jews now lived in the Diaspora (outside the Promised Land), a small Jewish population survived in Palestine, which, following the division of Rome into eastern and western kingdoms in 395, was ruled by the Eastern Roman, or Byzantine, Empire, which by then was Christian. Dubbing Palestine the Holy Land because it was there Jesus Christ had lived and, they believed, ascended to heaven, Byzantine rulers ordered the construction of numerous churches there and made Christianity the official religion of the region.

ISLAM COMES TO PALESTINE

By the third century of Byzantine Roman rule in Palestine, a dynamic new spiritual movement had burst upon the Middle East—Islam. Born in the early seventh century in the Arabian Peninsula, Islam is based on the teachings of Muhammad. Muhammad said that God spoke to him through an angel, commanding him to spread the message that there is but one God—Allah—and Muhammad is his Prophet. In time, Allah's revelations to Muhammad were written down in the Koran,

Islam's sacred book. Much more than a theology, Islam touches on all aspects of family and community life, including legal practices, manners, diet, and clothing.

By Muhammad's death in 632, most of Arabia had embraced Islam. Fired by their new faith, the Arabs exploded out of their homeland to spread Islam throughout the Middle East and beyond. In 634, Arab-Muslim armies swept into the Holy Land and within a few years had wrested control of the region from the Byzantine Romans. Gradually, the majority of Palestine's population adopted Islam along with the Arabic language.

The Arab conquest brought improved conditions for Palestine's small Jewish community, at least in some regards. Prohibited by their Byzantine overlords from residing in Jerusalem, under Arab rule Jews were once again allowed to live in their holiest city and worship at their central shrine, the Western Wall—all that remained of the Temple after the Romans torched it during the first Jewish rebellion. Although neither Jews nor Christians in Palestine enjoyed equal political and legal rights with the Muslim majority, both groups were allowed to practice their religions freely. This tolerant attitude was founded on the Muslim belief that the Judeo-Christian scriptures contain Allah's earliest revelations to humankind, before he spoke through an angel to his final and chief prophet, Muhammad.

Aside from the Age of the Crusaders, when European armies tried to conquer the Holy Land in the name of Christianity, the region remained under Muslim rule for the next 1,300 years. From 1516 on, the Muslim power in control of Palestine was the Turkish Ottoman Empire, which eventually ruled most of the Middle East. Although the Turks sent governors to administer Palestine, they did not settle in the colony in substantial numbers. Consequently, Palestine remained overwhelmingly Arabic in language and culture throughout the long Ottoman rule.

ANTI-SEMITISM AND THE FIRST ZIONISTS

The scattering of the Jews in the lands of the Diaspora after the 132–135 revolt against Rome did not sever their ancient tie to their spiritual home. Wherever the exiled Jews settled—whether elsewhere in the Middle East, North Africa, or Europe—they nurtured their beliefs and traditions, including their age-old devotion to the Promised Land, even as they strove to create a niche for themselves and their descendants in their new countries. Every year during the Passover rituals commemorating the Israelites' escape from slavery in Egypt, Jews throughout the Diaspora prayed to celebrate "next year in Jerusalem." For most, however, the reestablishment of a Jewish homeland in faraway Palestine must have seemed little more than a daydream.

In truth, many Jews probably had scant desire to go back to the land of their forebears, even if they thought such a return was actually possible. Over the centuries following their expulsion from the Promised Land, numerous Jews, especially those living in Western Europe, eventually came to enjoy a wide range of professional and educational opportunities in their new homes and prospered.

In other parts of the Diaspora, and particularly in Eastern Europe where the majority of the world's Jewish population had ended up by the nineteenth century, the Jews' experience had been very different. All too often, they faced isolation and persecution in their adopted countries. During the last decades of the nineteenth century, the lives of many Eastern European Jews had become more difficult than ever, as an especially virulent, state-sponsored anti-Semitism burgeoned in the region and thousands lost their lives in pogroms—organized raids on Jewish communities. In this climate of fear and violence, great numbers of Jews fled Eastern Europe, most for the United States. Others, however, came to believe that the only true haven for their people from oppression was a sovereign Jewish state, a state most assumed should be created in the biblical land of Israel and Judah. Zionism was the name given to this new movement for establishing a Jewish nation in Palestine, or Eretz Yisrael (the land of Israel), as the Zionists called it.

By the early 1880s, a small but determined group of Zionists had begun settling in Palestine. Much of this earliest wave of Zionist immigration—known as the First Aliyah (Hebrew for "ascension to Zion")—consisted of Russian students in their late teens or early twenties. They hoped that by purchasing land and setting up self-supporting agricultural communities, they could establish a foothold in the land of their forebears and serve as a vanguard for the rest of their persecuted brothers and sisters back in Eastern Europe. Although they had little money and no previous farming experience, they intended to survive by pooling their resources and the sweat of their brows.

The idealistic young immigrants were unprepared for the hardships and perils awaiting them in their Promised Land. Their ignorance of farming, their susceptibility to malaria and other illnesses, and the suspicion and even hostility with which their Arab Palestinian neighbors received them, created daunting challenges for the pioneers.

At the root of the animosity many Arab Palestinians exhibited toward the new Jewish settlers was land. Some of the land purchased for the First Aliyah farming communities was in uninhabited swampy areas, which the new settlers had to laboriously drain before cultivating it. Much of the rest of their land was obtained from absentee Arab-Palestinian owners. Before selling their land to the Zionists, the well-to-do owners, most of whom resided in cities far from their holdings, had rented it to groups of Arab peasants who built their homes, raised crops, and grazed their livestock on the property.

As more and more land was sold to Zionists by profit-seeking absentee landlords, tensions escalated between displaced Arab peasants and the Jewish settlers whom they blamed for their misfortunes. In 1886, just four years after the First Aliyah began, violence erupted between Arabs and Jews in Palestine. That year a peasant mob, furious because the land they had long inhabited had been sold to Zionists, attacked the Jewish farming settlement of Petach Tikvah. Four settlers were wounded before Ottoman troops intervened.

Known as the "father of modern Zionism," Theodore Herzl focused international attention on the Zionist movement, garnering support and funds for the cause. In 1949, one of the earliest acts of the new Israeli government would fulfill Herzl's dying wish to be buried in the newly established country.

THEODOR HERZL AND THE GROWTH OF ZIONISM

An even more pressing problem for the Zionist pioneers than skirmishes over land was the meager support their undertaking had attracted from the international Jewish community, with the notable exception of the French philanthropist, Baron Rothschild, whose contributions kept many of the early settlements afloat. The fledgling Zionist enterprise desperately needed additional outside financial backing to succeed. Largely through the remarkable leadership of one man—the Jewish-Hungarian journalist Theodor Herzl—the Zionist quest for a homeland in Palestine would attain unprecedented international attention and assistance as the nineteenth century drew to a close.

Herzl had long assumed that Jewish assimilation (absorption) into European culture would eventually cause anti-Semitism to fade away. By the mid-1890s, however, he had become alarmed by growing anti-Semitism not only in the eastern part of the continent, but also in Western Europe where the Dreyfus Affair, in which a French Jewish army officer was erroneously convicted of treason, had stirred up anti-Jewish sentiment in the press and among the general public. Herzl came to believe that the only solution to anti-Semitism was for Jews to form their own sovereign state.

In 1896, Herzl set down his arguments for Jewish nationhood in a widely read book entitled *The Jewish State*. Addressing his fellow Jews, Herzl wrote:

> We are a people—one people. . . . Oppression and persecution cannot exterminate us. No nation on earth has survived such struggles and suffering as we have gone through. . . . No one can deny the gravity of the situation of the Jews. Wherever they live in perceptible numbers they are more or less persecuted. . . . Let us first settle the point of staying where we are. Can we hope for better days, . . . can we wait in pious resignation till the princes and peoples of this earth are more mercifully disposed towards us? I say that we cannot hope for

a change in the current of feeling. . . . The nations in whose midst Jews live are all either covertly or openly Anti-Semitic. . . . Let the sovereignty be granted us over a portion of the globe large enough to satisfy the rightful requirements of a nation; the rest we can manage ourselves. Yes, we are strong enough to form a State, and, indeed, a model State. We possess all human and material resources necessary for the purpose.

Building on the interest generated by *The Jewish State*, in 1897 Herzl organized the First Zionist Congress in Basel, Switzerland, to discuss how to translate his ideas regarding Jewish statehood into reality. The highly publicized Congress attracted widespread Jewish support for Zionism throughout Europe, and particularly in Eastern Europe, from which the first small groups of Zionist settlers had emigrated to Palestine more than a decade earlier.

By the time of Herzl's death in 1904, his media savvy and organizational skills had helped to shape Zionism into a movement of worldwide importance. Financially, the Zionist enterprise was on more solid ground than ever before with the creation of the Jewish National Fund to buy land and promote settlement in Palestine. Fund-raising was carried out throughout the Diaspora but was especially effective in the United States, Great Britain, and the Austro-Hungarian Empire. Money flowed in not only from wealthy contributors but also from hundreds of thousands of ordinary Jews, including countless children.

Despite his success in winning popular and financial support for the Zionist cause, at the time of his death Herzl had failed to secure the diplomatic recognition he was convinced was also crucial to the establishment of a Jewish state in Palestine. After the Turkish Ottoman government, which was unwilling to promote the establishment of a Jewish state in the midst of its Muslim empire, refused to negotiate with him, Herzl tried unsuccessfully to obtain official recognition for Jewish claims in Palestine from several different Western powers.

THE SECOND ALIYAH AND ITS ACHIEVEMENTS

Although their enterprise still lacked the diplomatic backing Herzl believed was essential to the creation of a viable Jewish state, by Herzl's death in 1904 a new wave of Jewish immigrants had begun pouring into Palestine. During the Second Aliyah, the surge of Zionist immigration to Palestine from 1905 to the outbreak of World War I in 1914, some 40,000 Jews arrived in the Holy Land, about twice as many as had come during the First Aliyah.

As in the First Aliyah, the majority of these new immigrants were young Eastern Europeans. What distinguished the

While some Jewish communities concentrated on cooperative farming, others whose members were more accustomed to city life created settlements like Tel Aviv *(above)*. Literally meaning "Hill of Spring," the city was established on the Mediterranean coast near the ancient port of Jaffa in 1909.

immigrants of the Second Aliyah from their predecessors was their strong commitment to socialism, a system of social organization in which the ownership and control of all land, industry, and capital is given to the community as a whole.

Popularly known as Labor Zionists, the young socialists of the Second Aliyah stressed the importance of physical labor, especially farm labor, in building an independent Jewish nation. Convinced that Jewish settlers must do the work themselves, the Labor Zionists refused to hire Arab laborers, even though most of the new immigrants had been born and raised in the city and had no agricultural experience. Yet the question remained, how could an idealistic group of young urban intellectuals be refashioned into farmers?

In response to this dilemma, the Labor Zionists hit on the notion of the kibbutz (collective farm). On arriving in Palestine, immigrants with little money and farming know-how could head straight for a kibbutz, where they would be given housing, food, clothing, and plenty of hands-on agricultural training. In keeping with the Labor Zionists' socialist ideals, kibbutzniks (kibbutz members) worked together closely, sharing equally in the burdens and the profits of their enterprise. Everything was jointly owned, from houses and tractors to clothing, and everyone took a turn doing the various tasks of the kibbutz, from tilling the soil to cooking meals.

Another job shared by the kibbutzniks was standing watch against intruders. Since the early years of Zionist settlement, much Jewish property had been destroyed and many settlers killed during attacks by Arab neighbors, attacks that increased right along with Jewish immigration and land holdings during the Second Aliyah. In the face of these raids, some of the farmers of the Yishuv, as the Jewish community in Palestine was generally known, organized themselves into an armed defense force, the HaShomer (literally, "guard").

Notwithstanding the Labor Zionists' emphasis on working the soil, not all the Second Aliyah immigrants settled on kibbutzim or more traditional farms. Many headed straight for

Palestine's cities, particularly Jerusalem and the Mediterranean coast city of Jaffa. In 1909, another group, using money provided by the Jewish National Fund, established a new city near Jaffa on the shores of the Mediterranean—Tel Aviv. Boasting 2,000 Jewish residents by 1914, Tel Aviv was to become one of the Second Aliyah's greatest achievements.

During the final years of the Second Aliyah, Tel Aviv emerged as the center of a new movement that would significantly boost the sense of national identity developing among Palestine's Jewish population: the campaign to turn Hebrew, the ancient language of the scriptures, into the everyday tongue of the Yishuv. The founder and tireless promoter of the movement, Russian-born Eliezer Ben-Yehuda, was convinced that Hebrew would unify the Yishuv, whose members spoke a multitude of tongues, including Russian, German, and Yiddish (the language of many Eastern European Jews). When the Second Aliyah drew to a close in 1914, Ben-Yehuda's campaign had already made great strides: The Yishuv had a modern Hebrew dictionary, numerous Hebrew-language schools, and a thriving Hebrew press, and Hebrew was being spoken daily by tens of thousands of Jews in Palestine.

By 1914 much of the foundation had been laid for the establishment of a Jewish state in Palestine. A military tradition had begun with the creation of the defense force, the HaShomer, more than 40 agricultural settlements had been founded, as had the first all-Jewish city—Tel Aviv—and the Yishuv could now boast a population of some 85,000. Last but not least, the Jews of Palestine were well on their way to adopting a national language.

Yet, despite its many achievements, the Yishuv was still plagued by a number of grave problems, ranging from continued Arab resentment over Jewish land purchases—resentment that frequently spilled into violence against Zionist settlements—to the continued refusal of the Ottoman government to grant the Jews any autonomous area within Palestine. On the eve of World War I, the Zionists' ability to rebuild a viable Jewish state in their ancient Promised Land seemed far from assured.

3

A Disputed Land: Palestine from the First World War to the Second

The outbreak of World War I in 1914, in which the Allies (chiefly France, Russia, Great Britain, and the United States) fought the Central Powers (chiefly Germany, Austria-Hungary, and the Ottoman Empire), suspended Jewish immigration to Palestine. During the four-year war, Palestine's Jewish population not only ceased to grow but actually decreased because severely declining economic conditions led thousands of settlers to emigrate.

Because of Turkey's involvement in the conflict, World War I was fought in the Ottoman-held territories of the Middle East as well as in Europe. To cement the support of the Middle East's Arab leadership for the Allied cause, in 1916 the British government made a promise to Hussein ibn 'Ali. The patriarch of one of the Arabian Peninsula's most prominent families Hussein was the sharif and amir of Mecca, important spiritual and political positions to which he had been appointed by the Ottoman sultan. In a series of letters, the British high commissioner in Egypt (then a British protectorate) told Hussein that Great Britain would uphold Arab independence in the Middle East once the Turks had been defeated. Later, the question arose whether the Holy Land had been included in Great Britain's rather vague promises to Hussein regarding Arab autonomy in the former Ottoman territories, with the Arabs insisting it had, and the British claiming it had not.

In truth, British officials had quietly been making plans for bringing Palestine within their own sphere of influence from the war's beginning. As early as 1914, France and Great Britain secretly agreed to divide the Ottomans' Middle Eastern possessions between them after the war. Great Britain had strong strategic concerns in the Ottoman territories, and above all in Palestine. India was the British Empire's most valuable colony and controlling Palestine would help Great Britain protect a crucial route to India: the Suez Canal in nearby Egypt linking the Mediterranean to the Red Sea.

THE BALFOUR DECLARATION

While the British were promising independence to the Arabs on the one hand, and secretly negotiating with France for spheres of influence in Ottoman territories on the other, they further complicated the issue of what shape the postwar Middle East would take by involving themselves in yet another commitment regarding the region, this time with the Zionists. On November 2, 1917, the British Cabinet issued the Balfour Declaration announcing that "His Majesty's Government views with favor the establishment in Palestine of a national home for the Jewish people, and will use their best endeavors to facilitate the achievement of this object, it being clearly understood that nothing shall be done which may prejudice the civil and religious rights of existing non-Jewish communities in Palestine." In effect, Great Britain promised the Zionists it would back their efforts to create a Jewish state in Palestine, as long as that goal could be achieved without compromising the rights of the region's other inhabitants, i.e., some half million Arabs. The Declaration failed to explain just how those seemingly contradictory aims could be accomplished. Historians have long debated Great Britain's reasons for publishing the Balfour Declaration. Many contemporaries

The Balfour Declaration was named after the British politician Arthur Balfour, *(above, waving)* who negotiated with the World Zionist Organization. The declaration was a public statement by Great Britain pledging support and assistance in the creation of a Jewish homeland in Palestine.

viewed the proclamation as the government's way of thanking the chemist Chaim Weizmann, a leading European Zionist, for his valuable scientific research on behalf of the British military during the war.

Whatever the British government's motives may have been in issuing the Balfour Declaration, in November 1917 the Zionists were jubilant: At last a country—and not just any country but one of the world's leading powers—had agreed to support the creation of a Jewish homeland in Palestine. The Zionist cause had been given a huge boost, one that would have significant implications for Jewish immigration to Palestine after the war.

THE ESTABLISHMENT OF THE BRITISH MANDATE

Within a few months of the Balfour Declaration, British forces succeeded in wresting all of Palestine from the Turks. A new age was about to begin in the Holy Land—the era of British rule.

Following the surrender of the Central Powers in autumn of 1918, Great Britain, determined to hold on to Palestine as a strategic territory in any postwar division of the Ottoman Empire, maintained a large military force in the Holy Land. Two years later the continuing British presence in Palestine was given legitimacy by the new international peacekeeping organization, the League of Nations, which presented Great Britain with a mandate (order) to administer the region.

The mandate system was developed by the Allies at the end of World War I to help prepare the inhabitants of Germany's and Turkey's former colonies for self-government. In effect, Great Britain's mandate for Palestine entitled it to serve as trustee over the region until Palestine's inhabitants were deemed ready for the responsibilities and perils of independence. France also had mandates in two new countries carved out of the defunct Ottoman Empire by the Allies following World War I: Lebanon and Syria, Palestine's neighbors to the north and northeast.

In 1922, the League of Nations approved the final wording of the British Mandate over Palestine. To the Zionists' relief, the mandate committed Great Britain to honor the pledges made in the Balfour Declaration to create a Jewish homeland in Palestine. Many Zionists, however, were deeply disappointed that

Great Britain had decided to split its original mandate over the historic, biblical land of Israel (roughly what is today Israel, the West Bank, Gaza, and Jordan) into two. Palestine now occupied only the western portion of the original mandate, with some three-fourths of its eastern territory severed to create the Emirate of Transjordan. Direct British administration was to be maintained in Palestine, whereas Transjordan was granted qualified political independence under the rule of the son of Hussein ibn 'Ali, Abdullah.

GROWING ARAB-JEWISH TENSION

Encouraged by the inclusion of the Balfour Declaration in the British Mandate, Jewish immigration to Palestine rose sharply during the 1920s. Over the course of the decade, nearly 100,000 Jews, mostly Eastern Europeans, arrived in the region. By 1929, some 165,000 Jews lived in the Promised Land, comprising nearly 20 percent of Palestine's entire population.

The new immigrants, using money provided by the Jewish National Fund or private donors, significantly increased the Yishuv's land holdings. As during the earlier period of Zionist settlement before World War I, some of the land was purchased directly in small parcels from farmer-owners, but much was obtained from absentee Arab landlords. It is impossible to accurately gauge how many Arab peasants were displaced, but the plight of these uprooted tenant farmers received a great deal of attention from Arab nationalist groups, and articles denouncing the sale of land to Jewish immigrants appeared often in Palestine's Arab press. Nonetheless, the Zionists made good offers for the land, and numerous Arab landowners, whether motivated by pressing financial concerns or simply by the desire to make a profit, were more than willing to do business with the newcomers.

As the Jewish presence in Palestine grew during the 1920s, so did Arab hostility. By the end of the decade, Arab resentment regarding Zionist immigration had erupted in widespread violence. The immediate cause of the bloodshed was a long-standing conflict over Jewish and Muslim holy places in the Old City of Jerusalem, and particularly over the Western Wall. Sacred to Jews as the sole remnant of the ancient Second Temple, the wall and the area immediately surrounding it is also holy to Muslims as the place where Mohammed is supposed to have ascended to heaven.

In August 1929, the bitter dispute over the rights of Jewish and Muslim worshippers at the Western Wall boiled over into armed clashes when Arab mobs attacked Jerusalem's Jewish Quarter. The violence quickly spread to other cities and towns. In Hebron, just outside Jerusalem, more than 60 Jewish men, women, and children were killed and some 50 others wounded by Arab attackers.

After nearly a week of rioting, British troops finally managed to quash the disturbance. By then, 133 Jews and 116 Arabs were dead, with all but 6 of the Arabs killed by British soldiers. The high death toll forced the British government to reassess its policy in the Holy Land. An investigative commission was sent to Palestine from London, and in 1930 a white paper (British policy statement) was published, blaming the riots on Arab anger at Jewish immigration and land acquisitions. British administrators in Palestine had paid too little heed to the region's Arab inhabitants, who feared that the Jewish settlers would eventually submerge their own people in the region, the white paper suggested. In response to Arab concerns, it concluded, Jewish immigration to Palestine must be restricted and limitations placed on all future land sales to non-Arabs.

The Zionists felt betrayed. Chaim Weizmann, now president of the World Zionist Organization, and other influential European Zionists began a determined campaign to have the new policies revoked. After Weizmann convinced a number of key British politicians to protest the white paper, Prime Minister Ramsay MacDonald caved in to the pressure, and the new restrictions were dropped before they had a chance to go into effect. As it turned out, however, the Zionists' victory was destined to be short-lived.

THE ARAB UPRISING

During the 1930s, Jewish immigrants arrived in Palestine in unprecedented numbers. Many were Germans fleeing the alarming rise in anti-Semitism in their nation after Adolf Hitler's Nazi Party gained control of the government in 1933. These newcomers were different from the earlier Eastern European immigrants. Typically older and more established financially and professionally than their predecessors, the German immigrants included many businessmen, lawyers, engineers, and scientists who contributed much-needed expertise and investment capital to the young Jewish community in Palestine. In addition to the surge in immigration from Germany following 1933, immigration from Austria, Poland, Romania, Hungary, and Czechoslovakia also grew as fears spread of Nazi-inspired, anti-Semitic movements gaining power elsewhere in Europe. By 1936, Jews had come to make up nearly 30 percent of Palestine's total population.

Palestine's Arab community responded angrily to the new influx of immigrants. Still lacking political power and losing ever more of their demographic edge to the Jewish newcomers with each passing year, the Arab leadership judged it had absolutely nothing to show for supporting Great Britain during the First World War. The hopes for an independent and united Arab state they had nurtured during the war had changed to bitterness in the face of more than a decade of mandatory rule and nonstop Jewish immigration. All around them they saw other Arab countries like Transjordan and Egypt gaining more and more independence from the British, even as their own chances for an independent Arab state in Palestine seemed to be dwindling.

In an effort to force the British to halt Jewish immigration and land purchases and grant the establishment of an Arab national government in Palestine, Arab leaders proclaimed a general strike and a boycott of all British and Jewish goods in the spring of 1936. Before long, the Arabs' economic campaign moved toward large-scale armed conflict. Jewish businesses

The controversial formation of Israel was met by protests, boycotts, and violence from Arabs who had inhabited the area for generations. During riots in Jaffa, Arabs killed 17 Jews from Tel Aviv. *Above*, fellow Jewish citizens accompany the corpses of the 17 victims on April 26, 1936.

and farms were attacked and many Jews killed by Arab riot-
ers. The violence escalated as Jews fought back to defend their
lives and property. Determined "to suppress all outbreaks of
lawlessness," by October 1936 British troops had killed nearly
150 Arabs.

As Arab casualties rose, Arab resistance to the British administration hardened. Accusing them of placing Zionist demands
above the rights of the region's Arab majority, Arab Palestinians increasingly placed the blame for their plight on the
British. Police stations were bombed, military installations
sabotaged, and dozens of British officials and soldiers killed
by the rebels.

In an attempt to stop the bloodshed, Great Britain sent an
investigative commission headed by Lord Robert Peel to Palestine. In 1937, the Peel Commission published a report asserting
that cooperation between Arabs and Jews in a single Palestinian
state was unfeasible and recommending the partition of Palestine into separate Arab and Jewish states based on population.
Under the Peel Plan, the Jews would receive about 25 percent of
the territory and the Arabs most of the remaining 75 percent. To
protect Great Britain's strategic concerns in the region, the commission called for the British government to retain control over
major roads to the Mediterranean and the Red Sea. Jerusalem
would also remain under British rule.

Although most Zionist leaders were willing to consider the
plan, it was roundly condemned by Arab Palestinian leaders,
who refused to accept the creation of any Jewish state in the
region, even the small one the Peel Commission called for. All of
Palestine was their national territory, the Arabs contended, and
they did not see why they should be compelled to relinquish any
of it to a people whom they viewed as interlopers.

Meanwhile, the Arab revolt raged on. In 1939, British officials began using increasingly harsh measures to quell the
violence, executing dozens of convicted Arab rebels. By 1939,
thousands of people had died in the uprising, the majority of
them Arabs.

THE WHITE PAPER OF 1939

As the Arab insurrection was claiming ever more lives in Palestine, the German invasion of Czechoslovakia had brought Europe to the brink of war by the spring of 1939. Worried about the situation in their own backyard, British leaders sought to free themselves from the Palestinian quagmire as quickly as possible. Military reinforcements from home had helped to curb much of the Arab violence in recent months, but if war broke out in Europe, Great Britain could not continue to commit large numbers of troops to Palestine. As war drew nearer, the British were also becoming concerned that widespread Arab discontent with their handling of Palestine would push Arabs throughout the Middle East into the German camp. Should the Arabs side with Germany, Great Britain could lose access both to the Suez Canal, its lifeline to India, and to the Middle East's vast reserves of oil, an essential commodity for any modern army.

Determined to avert the resurgence of widespread Arab violence in Palestine during this period of uncertainty in Europe, in May 1939 the British published a new white paper imposing strict limitations on Jewish immigration to the region. According to the policy statement, only 75,000 Jews would be allowed into Palestine over the next five years, with Arab leaders having the right to approve all immigration into the region after that time. The white paper also called for the establishment of a single Palestinian state within the next decade, with Arab and Jewish representation in the government in proportion to population:

> The objective of His Majesty's Government is the establishment within ten years of an independent Palestine State in such treaty relations with the United Kingdom as will provide satisfactorily for the commercial and strategic requirements of both countries in the future. . . .
>
> Jewish immigration during the next five years will be at the rate which, if economic absorptive capacity permits, will bring the Jewish population up to approximately one-third of the

total population of the country. Taking into account the natural increase of the Arab and Jewish populations, and the number of illegal Jewish immigrants now in the country, this would allow the admission . . . of some 75,000 immigrants over the next five years. . . .

After the period of five years no further Jewish immigration will be permitted unless the Arabs of Palestine are prepared to acquiesce in it.

His Majesty's Government are determined to check illegal immigration, and further preventative measures are being adopted. The numbers of any Jewish illegal immigrants who, despite these measures, may succeed in coming into the county and cannot be deported will be deducted from yearly quotas.

The Zionists were incensed. How dare Great Britain restrict immigration to Palestine at a time when the Nazis were ruthlessly persecuting European Jews and nations around the world were slamming shut their doors to a flood of terrified Jewish refugees? Blasting the white paper as a betrayal of the pledges made to the Jewish people in the Balfour Declaration and the League of Nations Mandate, Zionist leaders demanded its revocation. Their complaints and demands went unanswered, however. Great Britain's leaders had made up their minds that Palestine's embittered Arab population must be appeased, even if that appeasement could only be accomplished at the Jews' expense.

THE BUILDING BLOCKS OF STATEHOOD

Although the Zionists suffered a serious setback with the adoption of the white paper of 1939, the Yishuv's position in Palestine on the eve of World War II was actually quite solid. For throughout the interwar years, Zionist leaders had worked diligently to furnish the Jewish community in Palestine with the trappings of nationhood, quietly assembling the political, military, social, and economic building blocks for future Jewish self-government.

According to the League of Nations Mandate, Great Britain was supposed to encourage Palestine's Jewish and Arab communities to manage their own internal affairs. By 1929, the Yishuv had formed an efficient protogovernment, the Jewish Agency, to direct all aspects of their economy and society. Among the various institutions overseen by the agency were schools, hospitals, agricultural settlements, and a powerful national labor confederation, the Histadrut. Founded by Labor Zionists inspired by the socialist traditions of the Second Aliyah, the Histadrut (General Federation of Labor) was dedicated to meeting the needs of the Yishuv's workers, including health care and housing. The Histadrut also helped create employment opportunities for Jews and improve the quality of life generally within the Yishuv by constructing roads, factories, and homes.

During the interwar years, the Jews were also quietly developing an underground army called the Haganah (Defense) to replace the smaller HaShomer organization. The Haganah recruited thousands of men and women throughout Palestine to defend their fellow Jews in cities and rural settlements, especially following the 1929 riots. During the Arab uprising of 1936–1939, Haganah members played an important role in protecting the people and property of the Yishuv.

Although Arab Palestinians were given the same opportunities to run their own internal affairs as the Jews were under mandatory rule, they were not as well organized or unified as their rivals, and consequently were far less successful at constructing the foundations of future statehood. While Arabs across Palestine were protesting—often violently—against Jewish immigration and land purchases and British rule generally during the 1920s and 1930s, they were neglecting to organize themselves into an effective political or military force. Traditionally, Palestine's overwhelmingly rural population had been organized around local, clan-based groupings. These strong tribal loyalties worked against Arab unity, playing a role in the failure of the 1936–1939 uprising against the British and, even more significantly, in the Arabs' inability to fashion the sort of sophisticated political, economic, social, and military institutions that the Yishuv had developed by the eve of World War II. Various Arab committees and political parties did spring up during the interwar years, but internal feuding severely undercut their authority and potency. By the end of the uprising in 1939, most of these groups lacked any leadership whatsoever, even a divided and squabbling one, as the majority of Palestine's nationalist leaders had been killed, exiled, or imprisoned by British authorities during the course of the rebellion.

Thus, in 1939, although outnumbered by the Arabs and saddled with harsh new immigration restrictions, the Jews were actually in a better position to establish and maintain a viable state in Palestine than their rivals. With the German invasion of Poland and the beginning of World War II in September 1939, however, most Jews in Palestine and throughout the Diaspora agreed that any efforts to establish that new state would have to be put on hold until Hitler and his violent anti-Jewish crusade could be vanquished.

4

The State of
Israel Emerges

With the outbreak of World War II in September 1939, Jewish spokesmen in Palestine and around the world suspended their vocal campaign against the white paper published just four months earlier. Leaders like Chaim Weizmann, president of the World Zionist Organization, and David Ben-Gurion, head of the Jewish Agency, were convinced that their chief responsibility was to support Great Britain and its Allies in the battle against Hitler. Their political fight against the white paper would have to be deferred until the Nazis were defeated.

Instead of publicly attacking the white paper, the Jews concentrated on quietly undercutting its effectiveness by smuggling refugees into Palestine from Nazi-occupied Europe. The Haganah, the Yishuv's underground army, took a leading role in this illegal immigration. They were assisted in their efforts by two small splinter groups, Irgun and Lehi. These right-wing militants had separated from the Haganah because they favored a more aggressive strategy against the Arabs and the British and because they disapproved of its close relationship with the socialistic Labor Zionists who dominated the Jewish Agency and the Histadrut. By the end of the war in Europe in May 1945, Haganah, Irgun, and Lehi volunteers had managed to sneak at least 20,000 illicit immigrants into the country, most of them on crowded, dilapidated ships.

A REBELLION AGAINST THE BRITISH

After Nazi Germany's surrender to the Allies in May 1945, the world finally began to grasp the scope of Hitler's brutal crusade against European Jewry. The statistics were shocking. Six million men, women, and children—about two-thirds of Europe's

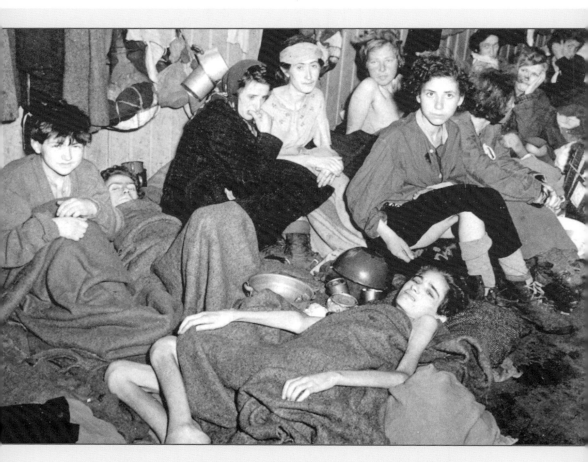

During World War II, Nazi Germany had expanded throughout Europe, rounding up entire Jewish communities along the way. People who were taken from their homes and businesses were placed into concentration camps, like this one in Bergen-Belsen, Germany. Millions were either quickly exterminated or worked to death. After the war ended, many of the survivors of these camps were hesitant to return to their former countries, instead hoping for a new home in British-occupied Palestine.

Jewish population—had been systemically slaughtered. Some 200,000 other European Jews languished in "displaced persons" camps in Germany, Austria, and Italy. Their loved ones dead, their homes and businesses destroyed or confiscated, many in the camps could not—or would not—return to their nations of origin. They hoped instead to try to rebuild their shattered lives in a new land—Palestine.

With the terrible facts of the Holocaust now exposed, many Zionist leaders assumed that Great Britain would open wide the gates of Palestine to the traumatized survivors of Hitler's "Final Solution." They were badly mistaken. Fearing a violent Arab response in Palestine and throughout the Middle East if it permitted unrestricted Jewish immigration to the Holy Land, the British government refused to rescind the strict quotas set down in the 1939 white paper. Even in the face of widespread censure from Europeans and Americans haunted by the Nazi death camps, the British government clung to its prewar immigration policies.

The British officials' unwillingness to expand Jewish immigration, combined with their failure to enunciate any definite plan for Palestine's future, infuriated the Yishuv's leadership. In response, the Haganah and the two right-wing splinter groups, Irgun and Lehi, continued to smuggle thousands of Jewish immigrants into the country in defiance of British law. At the same time, they also committed themselves to a bold campaign designed to end mandatory rule and oust the British from Palestine altogether. Determined to make life in Palestine untenable for the British, the Haganah, with the blessing of most of the Jewish Agency leadership, began targeting the British infrastructure, sabotaging railroad lines, bridges, utilities, and communications throughout the country.

Lehi and Irgun members adopted more brutal tactics to persuade the British to leave. Despite harsh criticism of their methods by much of the Jewish community, the two dissident groups targeted British officials and soldiers, carrying out numerous kidnappings and assassinations. In July 1946, Irgun terrorists bombed the King David Hotel in Jerusalem, head-quarters for the British administration's Criminal Investigation Division. Ninety-one people were killed in the blast, earning the Jewish dissidents negative publicity throughout the world. Although the Haganah and the Jewish Agency condemned the bombing, the Irgun- and Lehi-led terrorist campaign contin-ued. By 1947, Palestine's beleaguered British servicemen were being housed in fortresslike compounds encircled by barbed wire, while back in Great Britain, the heavy human and finan-cial costs of sustaining mandatory rule in the Holy Land were coming under increasing fire.

THE UNITED NATIONS PARTITION PLAN

Two years after the end of World War II, the war-weary British decided they had had enough of Palestine and its unremitting violence. Moreover, with the recent demise of British rule in India, Great Britain's central reason for remaining in Palestine—the protection of key routes to India and particularly of the Suez Canal—had disappeared. In April 1947, therefore, Great Britain announced it was relinquishing its mandate over Palestine. The official date for termination of the mandate and withdrawal of all British troops was set for May 15, 1948.

With Great Britain pulling out of the Holy Land, the dilemma of how to satisfy the national ambitions of Palestine's Arabs and Jews fell to the world's new peacekeeping organization, the United Nations. A UN commission comprising delegates from 11 nations was formed to investigate the situation in Palestine and recommend a plan for the country's political

(opposite) The United Nations Partition Plan of 1947 was welcomed by most Jews, since it gave them twice as much land as the British Peel Commission had been willing to award them ten years earlier. In sharp contrast, Palestine's Arab leaders, who continued to insist that Palestine must remain a single state, were incensed by the proposal.

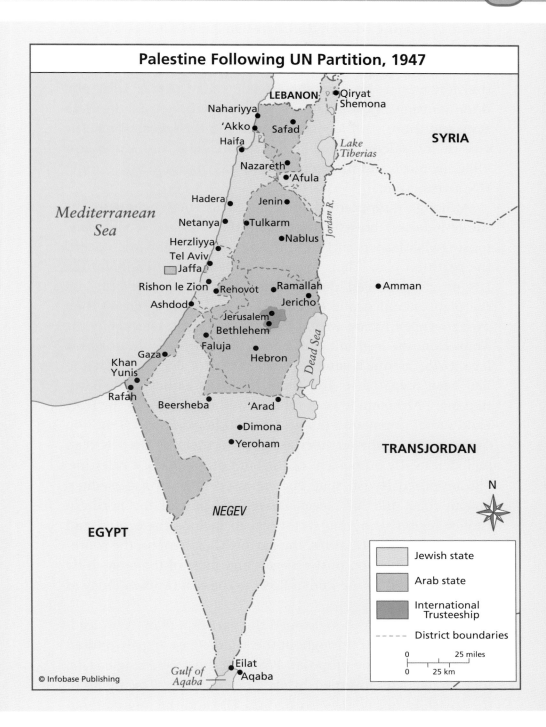

Palestine Following UN Partition, 1947

LEBANON

Qiryat Shemona

Nahariyya

'Akko

Safad

Haifa

SYRIA

Lake Tiberias

Nazareth

'Afula

Hadera

Jenin

Mediterranean Sea

Netanya

Tulkarm

Jordan R.

Herzliyya

Nablus

Tel Aviv

Jaffa

Rishon le Zion

Rehovot

Ramallah

Amman

Ashdod

Jericho

Jerusalem

Bethlehem

Faluja

Dead Sea

Gaza

Hebron

Khan Yunis

Rafah

Beersheba

'Arad

Dimona

TRANSJORDAN

Yeroham

EGYPT

NEGEV

N

Jewish state

Arab state

International Trusteeship

- - - - District boundaries

0   25 miles

0   25 km

© Infobase Publishing

Gulf of Aqaba

Eilat

Aqaba

future. Deeming cooperation between Arabs and Jews in Palestine to be impossible, the commission urged the country be partitioned into separate Jewish and Arab nations. Palestine's division was to be demographically based: Areas with predominantly Arab populations would be allotted to the Arab state and those with Jewish majorities to the Jewish state. The city of Jerusalem, sacred to Jews, Muslims, and Christians alike, would be administered as an international zone under UN jurisdiction.

Although disappointed with the exclusion of Jerusalem, the site of Judaism's holiest shrine, from the proposed Jewish state, most Jewish leaders in Palestine and around the world backed the partition plan. Their support was hardly surprising, for the UN proposal offered the Zionists a great deal. Not only did the plan unequivocally endorse the Jews' right to create their own sovereign nation within Palestine—a claim rejected by the Arabs from the beginning of Zionist settlement—it awarded the Jews twice as much land as Great Britain's Peel Commission had been prepared to give them ten years earlier in its partition plan. Although Jews numbered well under half of the Holy Land's total population (about 600,000 Jews versus 1.3 million Arabs in 1947), the territory assigned to them by the UN plan included nearly 50 percent of the land of mandatory Palestine. The proposed Jewish state encompassed most of the Mediterranean coast and the Negev Desert and part of the northern Galilee region. The Arab sector was to include the central and western portions of Galilee, the narrow Gaza Strip in the southwest, a small portion of the Negev, and most of the large, hilly region bordered by the Jordan River to the east (known today as the West Bank).

Whereas most Jews welcomed the partition plan, Arab leaders in Palestine and throughout the Middle East angrily refused to even consider the proposal. Palestine must be a single state, they contended, governed by its Arab majority. The rights of the Jewish minority, they assured the UN and the international community generally, would be respected in the unitary Palestinian nation they sought to create.

Arab protests notwithstanding, on November 29, 1947, the UN General Assembly passed resolution 181 supporting the establishment of separate Jewish and Arab nations in Palestine. Thirty-three member states voted in favor of the resolution, including the United States and the Soviet Union, the two emerging superpowers of the postwar world. Thirteen countries, including all the Arab and Muslim member states, voted against the resolution, with 10 countries, including Great Britain, abstaining.

The resolution's passage did not mean that the UN had just established two new countries in Palestine—an action the peacekeeping organization was not legally empowered to take. All the resolution actually signified was that international opinion strongly favored the creation of two separate states. No provision was ever made by the UN for enforcing Resolution 181. If a Jewish nation were indeed to be founded within the territory of Palestine, it was going to be up to the Jews themselves to establish and defend that state.

The Arab world's response to UN Resolution 181 made it abundantly clear that the creation and preservation of an independent Jewish state in the Middle East would pose a daunting challenge for the Yishuv. Blasting the resolution as a shameless effort on the part of the Western nations to assuage their guilt for failing to save European Jewry from Hitler, Arab leaders in the Holy Land and throughout the Middle East furiously denounced UN support for a Jewish state in Palestine. Palestine, the Arab spokesmen avowed, belonged to the Arab people who were the bulk of its population. On December 17, the Arab League—an association of Arab states including Egypt, Saudi Arabia, Yemen, Transjordan, and two states that had only recently attained their independence from French rule—Syria and Lebanon—announced it would unite with Arab Palestinians in opposing the UN partition, by military force, if necessary.

RENEWED JEWISH-ARAB VIOLENCE

Within hours of the passage of UN Resolution 181, armed violence erupted between Arabs and Jews in towns and settlements all over Palestine. Fighting was particularly heavy along the one major road connecting the proposed Jewish sector with Jerusalem, as Arab irregulars attempted to impose a blockade on the city's Jewish neighborhoods. For the most part, the British refused to intervene militarily, stopping the fighting in a few places only.

By the end of March 1948, the Haganah had started taking the offensive in their four-month–long conflict with the Arab Palestinians. The Jews' goal was to secure and consolidate the territory designated for them by the UN partition plan before the British Mandate ended on May 15. They realized that, once British troops had evacuated, the way would be cleared for a full-scale attack on Jewish forces by the regular armies of the Arab countries bordering Palestine to the north, south, and east. In preparation for their offensive, Haganah leaders recruited and trained thousands of new fighters, equipping them with arms secretly purchased from Czechoslovakia in defiance of a British ban on the importation of weapons into Palestine.

Soon the Haganah had gained control of dozens of Arab villages and towns within the Jewish sector, launching a mass exodus of Arab Palestinians from the Jewish-held territories. Whereas some Arab families were forcibly evicted from their homes and land by Jewish soldiers, particularly those in border areas, the majority of the refugees departed voluntarily although most thought their departure would be temporary. Fear appears to have been a central factor in the decision of numerous Palestinians to abandon their homes for Arab-controlled parts of Palestine or for neighboring Arab countries. This was especially true after April 9, 1948.

On April 9, 1948, an incident occurred in Deir Yassin, an Arab village overlooking the main road to Jerusalem, that profoundly alarmed many Arabs living in the portion of Palestine designated by the UN for the Jews. On that morning, members

A man walks past homes destroyed in the village of Deir Yassin by Irgun-Lehi forces. Rumors of Arab villagers harboring snipers had sparked an attack from the two Jewish military groups, resulting in the deaths of more than 100 people, including women and children. The incident caused many of the villagers to flee from the area.

of the paramilitary groups, Irgun and Lehi, attacked Deir Yassin as part of a campaign to reopen the central highway into Jerusalem and break the Arab blockade of the city's Jewish quarter. For some time, Arab snipers stationed in hillside villages above the highway had been firing on Jewish convoys carrying supplies to Jerusalem. Although the people of Deir Yassin had generally maintained good relations with nearby Jewish settlements, Irgun and Lehi leaders were convinced the villagers had been harboring some of the snipers. Accounts differ as to exactly what transpired at Deir Yassin on April 9, but when the smoke cleared, some 120 civilians, including many women and children, were dead, cut down by Irgun and Lehi fighters.

News of the massacre spread quickly through Palestine's Arab community. Although both the Haganah and the Jewish Agency immediately condemned the killings at Deir Yassin, in the wake of the bloodshed, Arab families fled Jewish-occupied areas in terror. There is no evidence that the Irgun-Lehi troops deliberately engineered the Arabs' panicky flight from their share of Palestine by killing civilians at Deir Yassin, yet the Arabs' mass exodus during the following weeks certainly worked in the Jews' favor.

In 1947, the year before the killings at Deir Yassin, some 350,000 Arabs lived alongside 600,000 Jews in the planned Jewish sector. By May 1948, tens of thousands of Arabs had left, increasing the Jewish majority significantly and opening more land for Jewish farms and towns.

THE CREATION OF THE STATE OF ISRAEL

With the termination of the British Mandate just days away, the Yishuv's leaders debated whether they should declare an independent Jewish state in the territory assigned to them by the UN as soon as the last British troops evacuated or delay their proclamation of nationhood until they could build up their military forces further. Everyone agreed that much was riding on this question, for Palestine's Arab neighbors had been threatening for months to intervene militarily if any attempt was made to establish a Jewish nation in the region.

Both Ben-Gurion and Weizmann agreed that a declaration of independence should not be delayed. "I dare believe in victory. We shall triumph!" Ben-Gurion assured his colleagues in the Jewish Agency. Ben-Gurion's dreams of victory over his people's Arab foes had some basis in fact. By the beginning of May 1948, Jewish forces had not only managed to gain control of the entire Jewish sector of Palestine but had also secured strategic positions in some territories within the designated Arab Palestinian sector, positions that could eventually prove useful as either offensive bases or defensive obstacles. Moreover, the political and economic underpinnings of the future Jewish nation in the form of the Jewish Agency and the Histadrut were solid, and despite the ongoing differences between right-wing groups like Irgun and the leftist Labor Zionists who dominated the Jewish quasi government, a deep feeling of national unity permeated the Yishuv. The time had come to try to make real the age-old dream of a revitalized Jewish nation in the Promised Land.

On the afternoon of May 14, 1948, just a few hours before the last British soldiers were scheduled to leave the Holy Land, David Ben-Gurion, as head of his new nation's provisional government, announced the establishment of the State of Israel. The creation of Israel had been authorized not only by UN Resolution 181, Ben-Gurion avowed, but also by the "self-evident right of the Jewish people to be a nation, like all other nations, in its own sovereign state." Almost immediately, the new state was formally recognized by the world's two leading powers—the United States and the Soviet Union. They were soon followed by most of the United Nations' other member states.

The decision of the United States government to recognize the new Jewish state came on the heels of a bitter argument between President Harry S. Truman and Secretary of State George Marshall. Marshall, along with most of the State Department and many diplomats in the United Nations, was convinced that the only way to avoid a long and destructive war between the Jews and their Arab neighbors was to place Palestine under a direct UN trusteeship. Moved by the plight of the Holocaust survivors in Europe, however, Truman rejected Marshall's advice and formally recognized Israel within minutes of Ben-Gurion's proclamation of independence.

THE FIRST ARAB-ISRAELI WAR

Within 24 hours of the proclamation of the State of Israel, the first Arab-Israeli War, or the War of Independence, as it is known in Israel, began. The nearly eight-month–long conflict was really a series of brief wars, interrupted by UN-sponsored cease-fires.

Pitted against Israel in the first Arab-Israeli War were the armies of no less than five Arab nations, chiefly Transjordan and Egypt, but also Iraq, Lebanon, and Syria. Yet these armies did not represent their nations' entire fighting forces, by any means. In all, they numbered perhaps 80,000 men. Uncoordinated military strategies, outdated weapons, and rivalries between various nations and ruling families hindered the effectiveness of this token Arab army in the campaign to destroy Israel. Lacking effective national leaders and institutions, the Palestinians they had come to assist had managed to throw together an even less credible fighting force, largely composed of disorganized and inadequately equipped village militias.

Meanwhile, in Israel, Ben-Gurion had formally united the Haganah and most of the Irgun and Lehi forces into a well-organized and disciplined standing army, the Israel Defense Force (IDF). Although estimates differ regarding the size of the IDF, many historians believe that it included some 80,000 fighters by late 1948 and at least 100,000 full-time male and female soldiers by the war's end in January 1949. At the outset of the war, the IDF was even less well equipped than the Arab forces, for obtaining arms under the watchful eye of the British administrators had severly challenged the Haganah. As the war dragged on, however, the situation changed dramatically as the IDF received a massive infusion of armaments from abroad, particularly from its earlier supplier, Czechoslovakia. (Although President Truman was sympathetic to the Israeli cause, Israel was unable to purchase military equipment from the United States, which had placed an arms embargo on the entire region in hopes of minimizing the bloodletting.)

Israel's better-organized and, by late in the war, better-equipped forces, combined with its citizens' enormous will to win, allowed the tiny nation to emerge as the victor in the first Arab-Israeli War by January 1949. Between February and July 1949, Israel and its Arab neighbors Egypt, Transjordan, Lebanon, and Syria signed separate armistice agreements brokered by the UN.

According to the armistice agreements, Egypt, Transjordan, and Israel would each keep the territory its army had managed to occupy during the war. No formal peace treaty identifying permanent borders between Israel and its neighbors was negotiated, however, for the Arab nations refused to participate in peace talks. All the Arab participants stressed that their approval of the armistice agreements with Israel did not amount to a formal recognition of the nation of Israel or its 1949 frontiers.

THE WAR'S AFTERMATH

With the fighting over, it was evident that the big losers of the first Arab-Israeli War were the Arab Palestinians. The narrow Gaza Strip, theirs according to the UN petition plan that had been vehemently rejected by the Arab world in November 1947, was now occupied by the armed forces of Egypt. Transjordan occupied the large West Bank area, which was supposed to have been the heart of Arab Palestine, according to Resolution 181, and its army showed no sign of leaving, despite objections from some Arab Palestinian leaders. The rest of what had once been mandatory Palestine now belonged to Israel.

About 135,000 to 150,000 Arabs remained within the State of Israel after the summer of 1949 and were awarded Israeli

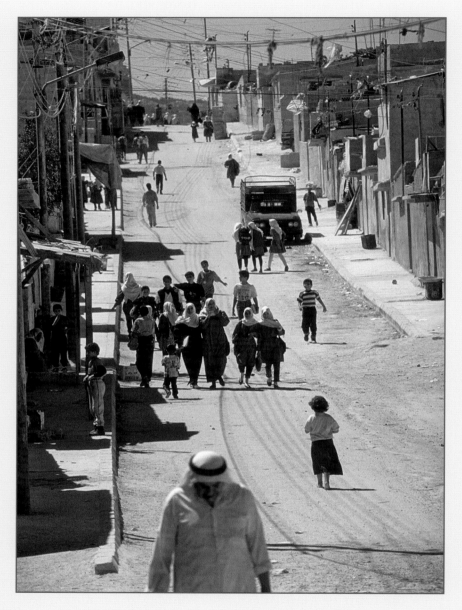

Palestinians displaced by the 1948 and the 1967 Arab-Israeli wars settled in refugee camps throughout the Middle East. Eighteen percent of Palestinian refugees live in 13 camps in Jordan, while others are distributed in cities throughout the kingdom. Here, Palestinians walk home through the Baqaa camp in Amman, Jordan, the biggest of all the camps.

citizenship. Some 700,000 other Arab Palestinians had become refugees by the end of the first Arab-Israeli War. Many had fled or been expelled even before the state of Israel was declared in May 1948; others left during the course of the war before the advancing Israeli army. The majority of the refugees went to the Jordanian-held West Bank or the Egyptian-held Gaza Strip, with most of the rest scattering in neighboring Transjordan, Syria, and Lebanon. Some ended up in existing villages and towns. Many more settled in refugee camps funded by the UN, which were designed to be temporary, but soon became permanent homes for hundreds of thousands of stateless Palestinians.

For Israel, in stark contrast, the first Arab-Israeli War was an impressive triumph. Not only was the new state able to hold its ground against a multinational invading force, it even managed to expand its area beyond the proposed UN borders of 1947, adding the whole of Galilee and the Negev, the western and southern sectors of Jerusalem (East Jerusalem and the Old City went to Transjordan) and a corridor of land connecting the Mediterranean Sea with Jerusalem. Still, the costs of the war for Israel were high—many of its most productive agricultural fields and citrus groves had been destroyed and its military debt was staggering. Far worse was the human toll: 6,000 Israelis—about one percent of the population—died in the violence that began directly after the issuance of UN Resolution 181 in November 1947 and lasted until January 1949. Tens of thousands of others were wounded.

By the end of the first Arab-Israeli War, the infant state of Israel had already endured a multitude of hardships and dangers. Many more trials lay ahead as the Israeli people struggled to build their new nation over the next decades.

5

Trials and Triumphs of the New Nation

O nce the first Arab-Israeli War was over, Israel's leaders focused on strengthening the foundations of the new state. Among the challenges they confronted were developing viable state institutions and a healthy economy, absorbing hundreds of thousands of new Jewish immigrants from a myriad of countries and cultures, and coping with the continued hostility of their nation's Arab neighbors.

SHAPING A WORKABLE GOVERNMENT

Overall, the transition from the quasi government of the Yishuv to an Israeli national government went smoothly. With the signing of the Israeli Proclamation of Independence on May 14, 1948, David Ben-Gurion simply traded his position as Jewish Agency chairman for that of chief executive of the new state's provisional regime. A cabinet selected from among his former colleagues in the Yishuv's government-in-waiting assisted him.

In January 1949, Israel held its first national elections. Twenty-one political parties competed for the 120 seats in the new national legislature or parliament, the Knesset, including moderate and left-wing socialist, centrist, and right-wing factions and Orthodox (religiously conservative) Jewish groups.

Under Israel's governmental system, voters cast their ballots for a political party, rather than for individual candidates. Each party compiles a ranked list of Knesset candidates. The overall number of votes a party wins determines how many of the men and women on its roster will serve in the Knesset.

No political party proved able to win an absolute majority of Knesset seats (61 of 120) in 1949, but the moderate socialist Mapai (Labor Party) garnered more seats than its rivals. As the most powerful party in the Knesset, Mapai earned the privilege of having its leader, Ben-Gurion, serve as Israel's founding prime minister. As Mapai head, Ben-Gurion would be re-elected to two additional four-year terms over the next decade, in 1955 and 1959. The Knesset chose Chaim Weizmann as Israel's first president, a largely ceremonial position.

Whereas the president holds little power in the Israeli state, the prime minister maintains a great deal, at least in theory. As chief executive, he or she selects a cabinet of up to 18 ministers (called a "government") at least half of whom must be Knesset members. The prime minister also sets the agenda for cabinet meetings, oversees the various Knesset committees such as foreign policy or education, and has the last say in all policy decisions. In practice, however, the prime minister's seemingly vast influence is limited by the nature of Israel's multiparty parliamentary system, as Ben-Gurion quickly discovered.

In the Israeli system, once a prime minister has chosen his cabinet, he is obliged to obtain a vote of confidence from the Knesset for his new government. This requires an absolute parliamentary majority. The prime minister and cabinet then remain in power only as long as they can retain the Knesset's backing—an absolute majority vote of no confidence at any time during the prime minister's four-year term will result in the fall of his government.

In common with every other Israeli political party down to the present, Ben-Gurion's Mapai could not win enough Knesset seats to make an absolute majority. Hence, to guarantee a working majority for his administration, Ben-Gurion had to form a coalition government composed of representatives from several parties. Ben-Gurion's political partnership aligned Mapai with smaller labor and centrist parties, and, although Ben-Gurion and most of the other coalition members were secular (non-religious) Jews, with Orthodox Jewish groups.

To preserve his fragile majority, Ben-Gurion hammered out political deals with the various members of his coalition and particularly with the vocal and determined Orthodox bloc. In

Pictured is an ultra-Orthodox soldier standing at attention. The first Israeli prime minister, David Ben-Gurion, made compromises to appease specific minority parties in his shaky government coalition. Ultra-Orthodox citizens, for example, are not required to serve in the military. Those who do choose to serve are provided with special accommodations, like male-only quarters and strict Kosher meals.

exchange for their support of economic and other measures Ben-Gurion considered of paramount importance, the prime minister made a series of concessions to his Orthodox supporters. By law, all Israeli businesses, public transportation, and governmental offices were to be shut down from sundown Friday to sundown Saturday in observance of the Jewish Sabbath, or day of rest. Tax revenues were to be used to support a dual system of religious and secular schools for Israel's youth, and some Orthodox Jewish students were to be exempted from compulsory military service—two concessions to the Orthodox minority that would attract increasing criticism over the decades from moderate and secular Jews. Finally, jurisdiction over "personal status" issues such as marriage, divorce, and burial were assigned to religious courts directed by Orthodox rabbi (Jewish clerics), which all Jews, even secular ones, were compelled to use. Members of the Christian and Muslim minorities were permitted to maintain their own religious courts for matters of personal status.

To secure his Knesset majority, Ben-Gurion gave in to the Orthodox on a number of important issues, but he would not compromise regarding Israel's constitution. Ben-Gurion and Mapai envisioned a national constitution based on secular and socialist principles, whereas the Orthodox bloc sought to make traditional Jewish religious law Israel's fundamental law. After extensive debate, the two groups finally agreed that the constitution be allowed to evolve over a number of years as the Knesset passed certain "basic laws" defining the organization of the Israeli government and individual rights. Although Israel still lacks a written constitution more than a half century later, the basic laws enacted by the Knesset through the decades effectively guarantee Israelis most of the same rights contained in the Bill of Rights of the United States.

A TIDAL WAVE OF IMMIGRANTS

One of the greatest challenges facing the new Israeli government was the absorption into the state of an avalanche of Jewish

Immigration to Israel by Country, 1948–2006

Year	Total	Former Soviet Union	North America	France	Great Britain	Argentina	South Africa	Ethiopia
1948	101,828	1,175	336	640	501	62	178	40
1951	175,279	196	618	401	347	325	72	1
1954	18,491	30	349	201	181	398	73	13
1957	72,634	1,324	313	267	223	665	96	5
1960	24,692	1,923	462	371	268	337	154	3
1963	64,489	314	968	546	536	4,255	409	17
1966	15,957	2,054	826	700	351	664	301	21
1969	38,111	3,019	6,419	5,292	1,763	1,274	715	14
1972	55,888	31,652	6,034	2,356	1,030	2,598	605	40

1975	20,028	8,531	3,065	1,382	707	892	415	19
1978	26,394	12,192	3,285	1,302	1,005	1,960	1,403	37
1981	12,599	1,770	2,670	1,430	882	949	220	650
1984	19,981	367	2,827	1,539	786	841	281	8,327
1987	12,965	2,096	1,986	888	577	1,078	737	231
1990	199,516	185,227	1,546	864	488	2,045	175	4,121
1993	76,805	66,145	2,280	1,372	647	375	437	863
1996	70,919	59,048	2,262	1,870	547	1,370	299	1,411
1999	76,766	66,848	1,697	1,366	383	936	228	2,290
2003	23,226	12,383	1,873	1,789	330	1,371	88	3,029
2006	19,269	533	2,095	1,781	506	299	139	3,595

Source: Israel Central Bureau of Statistics

immigrants. The first group to arrive in Israel following independence consisted of 25,000 illegal immigrants interned by British authorities in detention camps on the island of Cyprus. Soon after, Holocaust refugees from displaced-persons camps in Germany, Austria, and Italy and from Central and Eastern European countries such as Romania, Poland, Bulgaria, and Yugoslavia began flooding into the country. Hundreds of thousands of refugees also flocked to Israel from Jewish communities in the Middle East and North Africa, where many had suffered persecution at the hands of their Arab-Muslim compatriots in the wake of the Arab-Israeli War. Within four years of independence, approximately 700,000 Jewish immigrants had arrived in the infant state, more than doubling Israel's Jewish population of May 1948.

The Israeli government enthusiastically promoted this in-gathering of Jews from around the world. One of the Knesset's first acts was to open Israel's frontiers to unrestricted entry by all Jews. According to the Law of Return, every Jew who settled in the nation was automatically guaranteed Israeli citizenship. A variety of considerations motivated Israel's leaders to foster this virtually unrestricted Jewish immigration. Bringing the oppressed Jews of the Diaspora "home" to their biblical Promised Land had been the central goal of the Zionist movement from its founding in the nineteenth century. In addition to a deeply felt desire to fulfill the Zionists' dream of making the nation a sanctuary for persecuted Jews everywhere, Israel's leaders also had practical reasons for wanting to build up the nation's Jewish population. Compelled to share nearly 800 miles of borders with hostile Arab neighbors, Israel urgently needed additional man- and womanpower to maintain a large national army and to help create farms and towns in sparsely populated frontier areas.

Consequently, the Israeli government sent emissaries to countries with significant Jewish populations in Europe, the Middle East, and North Africa to encourage and expedite immigration to the nation. It also solicited funds from Jews around the world to help pay the expenses of transporting would-be Israelis home by land, sea, or air. Two of the most ambitious of these immigration projects involved the Jews of Yemen, on the tip of the Arabian Peninsula, and Iraq's large Jewish community. Massive airlifts were organized to bring nearly the entire Jewish populations of these two Arab nations to Israel—more than 150,000 men, women, and children in all. Jews from a multitude of other Middle Eastern and North African countries including Morocco, Algeria, Libya, Turkey, Iran, Syria, and Egypt were also encouraged by Israeli agents to settle in the new state.

By the end of 1956, Israel's population had almost tripled, reaching nearly 1,700,000. The government's goal of rapidly building up the population had been achieved, yet the young state lacked the resources to comfortably absorb so many new citizens. Although the national government and the Histadrut (General Federation of Labor) did what they could to provide the newcomers with food, housing, and medical care, and eventually with jobs and schools, the nation struggled to meet the needs of its swelling population. In large part, the first wave of immigrants from the Cyprus detention camps and Europe were housed in homes and buildings vacated by Arab Palestinians who fled or were driven from the country during and directly before the Arab-Israeli War. As the immigration continued unabated, however, other forms of shelter were urgently required. In response, the government hastily constructed a number of "reception camps" throughout Israel. At the camps immigrants ate their meals in crowded, communal dining areas and slept in crude canvas tents or aluminum huts until they could obtain employment and permanent housing.

ETHNIC TENSIONS

Of the various immigrant groups who arrived during the first decade following independence, the Middle Eastern and North African immigrants had the hardest time being integrated into Israel's society and economy. Ashkenazi Jews—as European Jews are known—were more quickly accepted by the Eastern and Western Europeans who comprised the majority of Israel's population in the 1940s and 1950s and dominated its political and educational systems. Consequently, most of the Holocaust refugees adjusted relatively rapidly to their new homeland and were soon able to secure productive livelihoods and decent housing. But the Oriental, or Mizrachi, Jews, as the Middle Eastern and Northern African Jews are commonly called, came from cultures that many Ashkenazi Israelis found alien and backward. Typically less educated and skilled than their European counterparts, Middle Eastern immigrants had more difficulty graduating out of the reception camps and into well-paying jobs and permanent accommodations.

During the 1950s, the Ashkenazi-dominated government struggled with the dilemma of where to settle the huge influx of largely uneducated and unskilled Oriental Jews. By the middle of the decade, it was placing many of them, and particularly the large Moroccan group that arrived in Israel during this time, in specially constructed transit camps on the outskirts of industrial areas where low-paying factory jobs were available. While most immigrants eventually made the transition out of the camps and into full-time work, others stayed on, either unable or unwilling to improve their lot. Consequently, some transit camps evolved into permanent urban slums, inhabited almost entirely by Oriental Jews.

In addition to placing Oriental Jews in transit camps near industrialized areas, the Israeli government assigned tens of thousands to agricultural "development towns" in thinly populated frontier areas. Often founded in regions with difficult climates or undesirable terrain, such as along the edge of the Negev Desert, the development towns stemmed from one of Ben-Gurion's earliest national defense policies—populating exposed border areas as a means of fortifying Israel's frontiers.

Typically separated into different towns, urban neighborhoods, and schools, all too often intolerant of one another's cultural traditions, the Oriental and Ashkenazi Jews found little aside from the two to three years of compulsory military service all adult Israelis shared to bring them together during the early years of statehood. It would take decades before the Oriental Jews felt fully assimilated into Israeli society and began to attain a level of economic, political, and educational success comparable with that of their Ashkenazi compatriots.

BUILDING THE ECONOMY

While the government strove to cope with the tidal wave of immigrants from many different lands, they were also struggling to strengthen Israel's faltering economy. Immediately after Israel declared independence, the Arab world imposed an economic boycott on the new nation, forbidding all trade between their citizens and the Israelis. Combined with the massive military debts Israel accumulated during the war of 1948, the ongoing costs of policing its borders, and the financial burden of housing and feeding the massive influx of new immigrants, the boycott had a devastating effect on the Israeli economy.

In response to the economic pressures confronting the country, the government launched a national austerity program, rationing such essential items as food and gasoline. The unpopular austerity measures were soon discarded, however, when foreign capital began to trickle into the country in the early 1950s from Jewish communities around the world and from the United States and other Western governments. Another vital source of funds during this period was the millions of dollars in German war reparation payments awarded to Israel in compensation for European Jewish properties confiscated by the Nazis. Government leaders carefully invested these funds in agriculture, technology, mining, and industry, and in the country's infrastructure, expanding and modernizing Israel's ports, railroads, and electrical generating capacity.

One of the government's most ambitious public works projects was the construction of the National Water Carrier, a massive network of pipes designed to carry water from the Sea of

Galilee in northern Israel to the farms of the Negev Desert in the south. Another major undertaking was the building of a nuclear facility in the Negev at Diamona to produce atomic weapons with the assistance of France, Israel's chief ally and arms supplier during the immediate postwar era. To this day, however, the Israeli government has never officially admitted to possessing nuclear weapons.

By the mid-1960s, a diverse array of Israeli industries including diamond polishing, chemicals, metal products, and food processing flourished, and although the Arab boycott remained in effect, Israel's international trade had expanded enormously. Israel's standard of living was still low compared to the most prosperous Western nations, yet was showing steady improvement. With the growth in industry and trade and the nation now agriculturally self-sufficient, two decades after independence the majority of Israelis were gainfully employed, reasonably well housed, and eating adequately.

THE SUEZ-SINAI WAR: THE SECOND ARAB-ISRAELI WAR

As Israel's leaders tried to focus on building the economy and other pressing domestic concerns during the postwar years, tension between Israel and its Arab neighbors remained a major distraction. Efforts to transform the armistice agreements of 1949 into peace treaties proved unsuccessful. Israel's Arab opponents refused to enter into peace negotiations until Israel allowed the hundreds of thousands of Palestinian refugees to return to their homes and retreated to the boundaries of the UN partition plan of 1947. Citing national security concerns, Israel adamantly rejected both of these demands.

Hostility and suspicion between Israel and the Arab powers were nurtured by the periodic border clashes that began immediately after the armistice agreements were signed. Palestinian guerrillas launched regular attacks on Israeli civilian and military targets from Syria's Golan Heights, from the West Bank, which was officially annexed by Jordan (formerly Transjordan) in 1950, and above all from the Egyptian-occupied Gaza Strip. Equipped and trained by the Egyptian government, Palestinian raiders made frequent incursions from the densely packed refugee camps of Gaza into Israeli territory. Hatred between Egypt and Israel intensified as Israeli forces retaliated against the Egyptian-sponsored raids, and a cycle of bloody attacks and reprisals ensued.

By the mid-1950s, Egypt had emerged as Israel's chief military threat from among its numerous Arab enemies. Under the leadership of the fervent Arab nationalist Gamal Abdel Nasser, Egypt built up its armed forces with Soviet assistance and launched a fierce propaganda campaign against both Israel and Western interference in the Middle East. In 1954, Nasser struck out at Israel by blocking its shipping through the Straits of Tiran, the nation's sole outlet to the Red Sea and its eastern markets. In July 1956, he struck out at the West by nationalizing the Suez Canal. Great Britain and France, who had long controlled the canal, were particularly incensed by Nasser's takeover of the strategic waterway.

France's and Great Britain's leaders decided the time had come to put Nasser in his place. Figuring that Israel would be only too happy to cooperate in their anti-Nasser conspiracy, they quietly sought Israeli cooperation for an invasion of the Sinai Peninsula and the Suez Canal Zone. In accordance with the three countries' secret pact, in October 1956 Israeli troops rapidly pushed into the Sinai all the way to the banks of the canal, where they were joined by British and French forces.

Israel and its allies had scored an impressive military victory in the brief Suez-Sinai War. They had also made a grave diplomatic blunder. U.S. President Dwight D. Eisenhower was incensed that he had not been consulted before the attack. Moreover, he feared the assault on Egypt might push Nasser further into the Soviet camp at a time when the Soviets and Americans were bitter rivals for influence throughout the world and particularly in the oil-rich Middle East. Eisenhower bluntly told the three countries to get out of the Sinai and instructed American officials to introduce a resolution in the United Nations censuring the conspirators' actions. Under heavy international pressure, Israel, France, and Great Britain evacuated the Sinai and returned all occupied territory to Egypt. In return, the United Nations agreed to place an emergency force in the Sinai to protect Israel's southern frontier from Arab raids and guarantee freedom of Israeli shipping through the Straits of Tiran.

The years following the Suez-Sinai War brought a temporary lull in Arab-Israeli hostilities. Yet despite Egypt's resounding military defeat in the Sinai in the autumn of 1956, Israel continued to view Egypt as a major threat to its national security, and with good reason. Nasser's popularity within his own nation and throughout much of the Arab Middle East burgeoned after the Suez-Sinai War. Even though he had suffered a humiliating loss at the hands of the Israeli army, Nasser had succeeded in nationalizing the Suez Canal, and Israel had been compelled to return all the territories seized in October 1956. With Soviet assistance, Nasser continued to arm his nation, paying particular attention to his fleet of combat planes, which he gradually built into the best military air force in the Arab world.

THE SIX-DAY WAR

In the spring of 1967, Israel's attention was focused not on Egypt, however, but on another Arab neighbor. Tensions between Israel and Syria over disputed areas on Israel's northern frontier had been mounting for some time. When Israeli counterstrikes failed to deter Syrian shelling of Israeli border areas, the government of Ben-Gurion's Labor Party successor, Prime Minister Levi Eshkol, announced it was contemplating more decisive military action. Rumors of Israeli troop buildups along the nation's Syrian border—which later turned out to be false—spread throughout the Arab community. As the self-proclaimed leader of Arab nationalism and the commander-in-chief of the premier Arab military force, Nasser felt compelled to act.

The successful—and surprising—end to the Six-Day War led to Israeli control of several new territories, including the Old City of Jerusalem, home of the Wailing Wall. One of the most revered sites in Judaism, this wall is the last remnant of the Second Temple, which was destroyed almost 2,000 years ago. When Israeli forces wrested control over the area, the first soldiers to reach the wall danced in celebration *(above)*.

In May 1967, Nasser demanded the immediate removal of the UN Emergency Force from the Sinai and began massing Egyptian troops on the Israeli-Egyptian frontier. He also reestablished his blockade on Israeli shipping through the Straits of Tiran, violating the terms of the UN-sponsored cease-fire agreement that had ended the Suez-Sinai War 10 years earlier. Soon after, Nasser signed mutual defense pacts with Syria, Jordan, and Iraq.

Convinced that an attack was looming, Eshkol and Defense Minister Moshe Dayan, the commander of Israel's 1956 Sinai campaign, decided to act first. On June 5, 1967, Israel's air force carried out a bold preemptive strike, demolishing virtually the entire Egyptian air force on the ground in less than three hours. Similar Israeli bombing raids would soon destroy much of the Syrian and Jordanian air forces as well.

Between June 5 and June 8, Israeli ground forces fought their way across the Sinai Peninsula to the banks of the Suez Canal in a lightning campaign, all but annihilating the Egyptian army as it attempted to retreat. Meanwhile, in the east, Jordanian forces shelled Israeli-occupied West Jerusalem, prompting Israel to launch an attack against the West Bank and East Jerusalem, both ruled by Jordan since 1950. As in the Egyptian campaign, the Israeli forces in the east won a rapid and overwhelming victory. By June 6, Israeli troops were in control of all Jerusalem, including the historic Old City and Judaism's central shrine, the Western Wall. By June 7, they had managed to secure the entire West Bank, all the way east to the Jordan River. That same day Israeli composer Naomi Shemer published her stirring ballad, "Yerushalayim shel zahav," ("Jerusalem the Gold"), in honor of the taking of the Old City, home to the revered Western Wall on the Temple Mount. Shemer's song soon became the anthem of the 1967 conflict in Israel:

We have come back to the deep wells
To the marketplace again.
The trumpet sounds on the Mount of the Temple
In the Old City.

In the caverns of the cliff
Glitter a thousand suns.
We shall go down to the Dead Sea again
By the road to Jericho.

In response to Syrian shelling in the north, on June 9 Israeli forces pushed into the strategic Golan Heights, just over the Israeli-Syrian border. By the next morning, the Israelis held not only the Golan but also the main road to Syria's capital, Damascus. The third major Arab-Israeli war since May 1948 was over.

On June 10, 1967, Israel, its three opponents, and the entire international community were stunned by the magnitude of the tiny nation's victory. In just six days of fighting, the IDF had inflicted humiliating defeats on the Egyptian, Jordanian, and Syrian armed forces, and on an expeditionary force from Iraq. Even more astounding, Israel had managed to more than triple its territory in less than a week, taking East Jerusalem and the West Bank from Jordan, the mountainous Golan Heights from Syria, and the Gaza Strip and vast Sinai Peninsula from Egypt. The Six-Day War, as the conflict of June 1967 came to be popularly known, would launch a new era of national pride for the Israeli people. It would also bring them a host of troubling new problems.

6

War, Peace, and the PLO

The Israeli victory of 1967 meant that the tiny nation was now in control of vast new territories and a vast new population of Palestinians—approximately 1 million of them in the West Bank and Gaza Strip. Israelis debated what to do with the conquered areas: Should they be traded back to Egypt, Jordan, and Syria for peace agreements or annexed and settled? Almost immediately, the decision was made to annex East Jerusalem and the Old City, the site of the Western Wall, and to declare a unified Jerusalem as Israel's capital. The Israeli government let it be known, however, that it was ready to exchange most, if not all, of the remaining conquered territory for peace treaties with its Arab neighbors.

This "land for peace" plan was at the heart of Resolution 242, passed by the United Nations several months after the War of 1967 in hopes of promoting a "just and lasting peace" in the Middle East. According to the UN resolution, Israel was to withdraw "from territories occupied" in June 1967 and the Arab nations, in return, were to "acknowledge . . . the sovereignty, territorial integrity and political independence" of Israel "and their right to live in peace within secure and recognized boundaries." The Arab states, however, rejected the territory-for-peace scheme, avowing that any direct negotiation with Israel would entail diplomatic recognition of the Jewish state, as unacceptable to them in 1967 as it had been nearly two decades earlier following the first Arab-Israeli War.

As hopes for a negotiated peace with the Arabs dwindled, more and more Israelis were inclined to hold on to the territories taken in June 1967. Many who advocated keeping the Gaza Strip, West Bank, Golan Heights, and Sinai Peninsula emphasized national security concerns. A return to pre-1967 boundaries made no sense from a strategic viewpoint, they argued, since it would put most of Israel's major cities back within artillery range of the nation's hostile neighbors. The territories, they maintained, provided a vital buffer for Israel against the implacable foes surrounding the country on three sides. Other Israelis cited religious and historic reasons for keeping the occupied territories, noting that much of the conquered area had once belonged to the Jewish kingdoms of biblical times. These proponents of "Greater Israel" advocated establishing a firmly rooted Jewish presence in the territories by developing and settling them.

Although the governments of Levi Eshkol and his Labor Party successor, Prime Minister Golda Meir, made no move to annex the territories, they insisted they would not withdraw Israeli troops from the occupied lands until peace treaties had been negotiated with the areas' former rulers—Jordan, Egypt, and Syria. As long as the Arabs adamantly refused to participate in peace talks, the Israelis gradually dug themselves deeper and deeper into the occupied territories, erecting paramilitary settlements around their strategic peripheries and developing their roads and other components of the transportation infrastructure. The government also began providing many of the territories' Arab inhabitants with health care and housing and encouraged them to take day jobs within Israel, especially in the booming construction industry for which the Palestinians provided a vast source of cheap labor. In time, the territories' utilities—including water and electricity—were connected to Israel's. Clearly, the manpower, infrastructure, and economy of the territories were becoming more and more integrated with those of the Jewish state.

Called out of retirement at 70 years old to become the new prime minister, Golda Meir dedicated much of her life to serving her country. Meir was dubbed "the Iron Lady" of Israeli politics nearly a decade before that epithet became associated with Great Britain's first female prime minister, Margaret Thatcher.

THE RISE OF THE PLO

Many Israelis viewed their nation's rule in the occupied territories as mild, even benevolent, arguing that occupation had brought unprecedented benefits to West Bank and Gaza Palestinians in the form of an improved infrastructure, increased employment opportunities, and superior medical care. The Palestinians themselves viewed the occupation very differently, however. One of the most important results of the 1967 War was the reawakened sense of national identity the conflict promoted among the Palestinian people, and particularly among the approximately 1 million who lived under Israeli military occupation in the West Bank and Gaza Strip. Under the rule of their fellow Arabs, the

Egyptians and Jordanians, the Palestinians of Gaza and the West Bank had endured their first 20 years of exile relatively quietly, failing to create a vocal or widely supported independence movement. Instead of focusing on the creation of a viable Palestinian state, the emphasis during those years had been on a Pan-Arab crusade against Israel generally, with other Arabs typically doing the talking for the Palestinians and discouraging the refugees from taking the lead in their struggle against the Jewish state.

After the Arab nations' stunning defeat in the War of 1967 and the humiliating imposition of Israeli rule in the West Bank and Gaza, however, many Palestinians came to believe that if they were ever to have a homeland, they had to take responsibility for their own liberation. No longer could they depend on other Arab nations to speak—or fight—for them. Founded in 1964, the Palestine Liberation Organization (PLO), a political body whose chief goal was the formation of an independent Palestinian state, took on new significance after June 1967. Under the determined leadership of the Palestinian exile Yasir (Yasser) Arafat, the PLO became a powerful umbrella organization uniting a number of Palestinian nationalist groups, including Fatah, a guerilla organization founded by Arafat in the late 1950s. Until 1970, when the PLO clashed with the royal Jordanian government, the Palestinian organization made its headquarters in Jordan, frequently harassing Israel on its border on the Jordan River. In late 1970, Arafat and the rest of the PLO leadership moved to Lebanon, where that nation's weak central government and ongoing battles between rightist Christian and leftist Muslim militia groups allowed the Palestinian organization to create a virtual state-within-a-state. From their bases in southern Lebanon, the PLO carried out terrorist raids against Israel's northern settlements, assaults that were inevitably followed by retaliatory Israeli shelling.

In addition to their border raids on Israel from Lebanon and other neighboring Arab countries, the PLO and a variety of militant Palestinian splinter groups engaged in a series of devastating terrorist acts against Israeli citizens outside as well as within Israel during the late 1960s and early 1970s. These highly publicized actions included bombings and airplane hijackings, including the May 1972 hijacking of a Belgian commercial airplane en route from Vienna to Tel Aviv. After hijackers landed the plane in Israel and demanded the release of 300 Palestinian prisoners, a daring IDF raid on the aircraft resulted in the release of all the passengers. On September 5 of the same year, the world watched in horror as Palestinian gunmen kidnapped and killed 11 Israeli athletes participating in the Summer Olympic Games in Munich, Germany.

THE ARAB-ISRAELI WAR OF 1973

While the terrorist tactics used by the PLO and other Palestinian groups were creating an atmosphere of anxiety and uncertainty among Israelis, the long-standing tensions between Israel and its Arab neighbors continued. Under President Nasser and his successor, Anwar Sadat, Egypt gradually rebuilt its devastated army with Soviet assistance, and engaged in a War of Attrition with Israel (1969–1970) in the Sinai in a costly and ultimately fruitless effort to regain the territory it had lost in 1967.

In 1973, a frustrated Sadat decided to launch an all-out attack on Israel with Egypt's ally, Syria, whose army had also been reconstructed with Soviet help after 1967. On October 6, on Yom Kippur—the holiest of all Jewish holidays—Egypt and Syria attacked Israel, taking the country's military and political leadership by surprise. Early that afternoon, 222 Egyptian warplanes launched a massive air strike against Israeli military targets in the Sinai Peninsula while 60 Syrian warplanes were simultaneously striking Israeli targets on the Golan Heights.

For a few days, Israel's very survival seemed at stake as Syrian and Egyptian armies pushed deep into the Sinai Peninsula and Golan Heights. Then the IDF, with the assistance of an extensive arsenal of sophisticated military equipment supplied by its chief ally since 1967, the United States, grabbed the offensive. Within three weeks, Israel had recaptured Golan and the Sinai, destroying much of the Syrian and Egyptian forces in the process. The fighting over, the United States helped broker a series of "disengagement" agreements between Israel, Egypt, and Syria.

THE TRIUMPH OF THE RIGHT

Although Israel ultimately repelled its attackers in October 1973, the war proved costly for the nation, both in loss of property and loss of life. By the end of the conflict, damage to private property and military installations on the Golan Heights, lost production, and military expenditures on planes, tanks, guns, ammunition, and fuel totaled $5 billion, and 3,000 Israelis were dead or missing, a stunning number for such a small country. The Labor coalition, or Mapai, managed to hold on to its parliamentary majority for several years following the war, but accusations that Prime Minister Meir and the rest of the Labor leadership had been caught napping by the Arabs in 1973 eventually caught up with the party. In 1977, after nearly three decades in power, the Labor Party fell to its right-wing rival, the Likud Party, headed by Menachem Begin (the former leader of Irgun during the War of Independence). In contrast to the Labor Party, which supports governmental control of the economy with limited free enterprise, Likud favors privatization of the economy. In foreign and security matters, it takes an assertive and nationalistic stance.

The Likud Party drew its support not only from Israelis disgruntled by the Labor government's failure to anticipate the devastating Yom Kipper attack but also from the Middle Eastern Jews who now comprised fully half of Israel's Jewish population yet still felt excluded from political leadership positions by the Ashkenazi-dominated Labor Party. Another integral part of the new Likud coalition was the religious right, which also sought a larger say in the government than they had previously been given.

Under Likud leadership, the government embraced a hard-line policy toward its Arab neighbors and began actively promoting

Home to over a million Palestinians, the Gaza Strip was occupied by Israeli forces during the 1967 Arab-Israeli War. The Likud Party urged Israeli citizens to build Jewish settlements in occupied territories like Gaza, creating entire Jewish neighborhoods like Neve Dekalim *(above)* in primarily Palestinian areas.

civilian settlements in the occupied territories. The government's rationale for encouraging settlements was that the new Jewish towns and villages would help solidify Israel's grip on the captured territory, most of which the right-wingers wanted to retain permanently as part of "Greater Israel." A handful of settlements founded by various Israeli citizen groups had already sprung up in the territories during Labor's rule. Under the aegis of the Likud, however, scores of new settlements were constructed in Gaza, and particularly in the West Bank, an area Begin and his supporters tellingly referred to by the biblical names of Judea and Samaria.

During the mid-1970s, there were fewer than 20 Jewish settlements in the West Bank, with a total population of about 5,000. By the early 1980s, 100 Jewish settlements existed in the West

Bank, with a total population of more than 20,000. Many of these settlements were established by religious nationalists, who contended it was the historic and spiritual destiny of the Jews to "redeem" or reclaim the ancient biblical lands of their forebears. Other new settlers, however, were motivated more by economic than ideological concerns, and particularly by the tax breaks, low mortgage rates, and other financial incentives offered by the Begin administration to any citizen willing to move to the occupied territories.

Yet as the Likud government was doing all it could to promote Jewish settlements in the occupied territories during the late 1970s and early 1980s, it was failing to put forth a clear plan regarding the future status of the territories or the rapidly growing Arab community inhabiting them. It seemed logical that the ultimate goal of the Likud's massive settlement program was annexation. However, annexation, particularly of the densely populated Gaza and West Bank territories, had many outspoken and powerful opponents both within and outside the Israeli government. The territories' large and rapidly multiplying Arab population, many Israelis feared, could not be united with Israel without fundamentally undermining the nation's Jewish character. Consequently, although Israel tightened its physical and administrative hold on the occupied territories during the late 1970s and early 1980s, Begin and the rest of the Likud's right-wing leadership made no effort to formally incorporate the lands into the Jewish state.

PEACE WITH EGYPT

Begin and his Likud Party were known for their hard-line approach to the Arab community. Yet soon after taking office, Begin surprised his supporters and detractors alike by making peace with Israel's most powerful Middle Eastern enemy for the past three decades: Egypt. It was President Sadat who initiated the peace process by approaching Begin in the autumn of 1977, apparently after coming to the conclusion that diplomacy was the only way to get the Sinai Peninsula back from the Israelis and end the expensive arms race between the two nations. Begin immediately invited Sadat to visit Jerusalem. He was not about to pass up an opportunity to make peace with his nation's chief

In September 1978, U.S. president Jimmy Carter brought together two old enemies, Egyptian president Anwar Sadat and Israeli prime minister, Menachem Begin, for a peace summit in Camp David in Maryland. Thanks in large measure to Carter's patient and skillful diplomacy, in March 1979 Sadat and Begin finally signed a formal Egyptian-Israeli peace agreement during a historic ceremony at the White House hosted by the American president.

rival and the first Arab country ever to show any serious interest in seeking an accord with Israel.

Sadat's historic trip to Jerusalem led to intensive negotiations between Egypt and Israel sponsored by U.S. President Jimmy Carter. Held at the U.S. presidential retreat in Camp David, Maryland, in September 1978, the face-to-face talks between Sadat and Begin got off to a discouraging start. After just three meetings, the two longtime enemies were barely speaking to one another. Determined to save the peace summit, Carter helped craft a detailed peace proposal and then volunteered to serve as a middleman between the Egyptian and Israeli leaders. Patiently shuttling back and forth between the two men, on day 13 of the summit Carter at last secured both Sadat's and Begin's approval for the plan.

In March 1979, Egypt and Israel signed a formal peace agreement during a ceremony hosted by Carter at the White House. According to the agreement, Egypt would regain all the Sinai Peninsula within three years in exchange for peace and the establishment of normal diplomatic relations with Israel. Most of the Sinai was to be demilitarized, with UN forces stationed there to guarantee continued compliance with the treaty. Although the Sinai had provided significant economic and strategic benefits to Israel over the years, Begin was willing to sacrifice the peninsula for peace with his nation's strongest adversary within the Arab world.

After March 1979, Israel immediately began dismantling its settlements and military bases in the Sinai. Yet, while the nation was making peace with Egypt and pulling out of the Sinai, it was achieving nothing toward cementing peaceful relations with Syria, its other opponent in the War of 1973, or with the increasingly embittered Palestinians. In 1981, Israel formally annexed the Golan Heights, ignoring repeated Syrian demands that the territory be unconditionally returned to them. During this period, the nation also tightened its grip on the West Bank and the Gaza Strip, erecting a number of new settlements there, despite the objections of the Palestinians and the disapproval of most of the world community, including Israel's staunchest ally, the United States. Although Arafat and the PLO enjoyed increased international recognition during the 1970s, Israel also adamantly refused to enter into talks with the PLO leadership regarding the future of the occupied territories or a return of Palestinian refugees to Israel. The PLO, the Israeli government insisted, was a terrorist organization and Israel did not negotiate with terrorists.

THE WAR IN LEBANON

Having dismissed the possibility of a political solution to the problem of the PLO and its ongoing terrorist activities, by the early 1980s the Israeli government had decided on a military solution. It would use its overwhelming military strength to go after the PLO in Lebanon, where the organization had made its headquarters since 1970 and from which it had staged incursions and launched missiles into northern Israel during the past decade. Following a PLO military buildup in southern Lebanon in 1982 and the attempted assassination of the Israeli ambassador to London by a Palestinian militant, Begin and his hawkish defense minister, Ariel Sharon, agreed that the time had come to strike. Their ostensible goal was to push all PLO forces from southern Lebanon, thus putting northern Israel out of the range of PLO artillery. The IDF did not stop at destroying PLO military bases in southern Lebanon, however. Instead, it pushed all the way north to Beirut, Lebanon's capital city and home to Arafat and much of the rest of the PLO's leadership.

Hesitant to send the army into Beirut, Sharon ordered the military to lay siege to the capital city in hopes of pressuring Arafat and other PLO leaders into fleeing Lebanon. For two months Israeli forces, using artillery shells and air bombardment, pounded PLO targets in West Beirut, headquarters for the organization and the site of several large Palestine refugee centers. Civilian casualties were estimated in the thousands and the long siege earned the censure of the world community and of many Israelis. Shortly after the Beirut siege ended in late August 1982, another incident drew even harsher criticism of Israel's military and political leadership.

In September 1982, Christian Lebanese militiamen allied with the Israelis massacred hundreds of Palestinians in two refugee camps near the capital city. The Israeli leadership, and particularly Defense Minister Sharon, should have anticipated the attack and shielded the refugees from their Lebanese enemies, many observers believed. Nearby Israeli forces did nothing to stop the killings and were even accused of abetting them. In the midst of a public outcry regarding Israel's complicity in the massacre, Sharon resigned from his cabinet post.

The Israeli invasion of Lebanon ended with a mixed outcome for the Jewish state. It was successful in that Arafat and his cohorts fled Lebanon for the North African country of Tunisia after Israeli forces vanquished PLO troops and their Syrian and left-wing Lebanese supporters. In 1985, Israel pulled its forces out of all but the southernmost area of Lebanon, where they remained for another five years to safeguard the Israeli border. Yet, if the war succeeded in forcing the PLO out of Lebanon, it failed to seriously weaken the Palestinian organization or to halt its terrorist acts or those of other militant Arab groups in Israel and the occupied territories. Moreover, the campaign had an extremely divisive effect on Israeli politics and society. The Lebanese war was the first military conflict opposed by a significant number of Israelis, and the nation's cities were rocked by massive antiwar demonstrations during the fighting. In 1983, dispirited by the controversial and costly conflict in Lebanon, Begin abruptly resigned, leaving Foreign Minister Yitzhak Shamir in charge of the government.

Weakened by its association with the unpopular war in Lebanon and by skyrocketing inflation at home, the Likud bloc failed to win a decisive majority in the 1984 elections, following nearly a decade in power. Since both the Likud bloc and the Labor coalition won virtually the same number of seats in the Knesset, Likud and Labor agreed to share the administration of the government, with Labor leader Shimon Peres and Likud leader Shamir trading off the posts of prime minister and foreign minister during the next four years. The closely contested 1988 elections ushered in another "national unity government" with Peres serving as finance minister this time, and Shamir as prime minister. The most pressing challenge facing Shamir and Peres and their national unity government was in the occupied territories of the Gaza Strip and the West Bank, where after 20 years of relative calm, Arab discontent with Israeli rule had now reached the boiling point.

New Violence and a Faltering Peace Process

With the PLO exiled to Tunis in North Africa and the number of Israeli settlers in the territories continuing to rise, the Palestinians living under Israeli military rule felt more isolated and powerless than ever. In late 1987, widespread unrest and frustration among the Arab inhabitants of the occupied lands finally exploded into a full-scale insurrection. Known as the intifada (Arabic for "shaking off"), the popular uprising started in the packed and squalid refugee camps of the Gaza Strip and soon spread throughout the West Bank and into the predominantly Palestinian sectors of East Jerusalem.

Although the intifada was spontaneous, it was also well organized and included daily demonstrations, strikes, commercial shutdowns, boycotts, a rock-throwing campaign by Palestinian children against Israeli soldiers, and numerous violent attacks against Israeli citizens, especially Gaza and West Bank settlers. The Israeli occupying army was stretched to its limits trying to contain the highly publicized uprising, which managed to draw an enormous amount of international attention—most of it negative—to Israel's two decade–long occupation of the West Bank and Gaza Strip. By the early 1990s, many Israelis had become convinced that a new way of handling the territories wrested from Jordan and Egypt in 1967 and their embittered and restive Arab inhabitants was desperately needed.

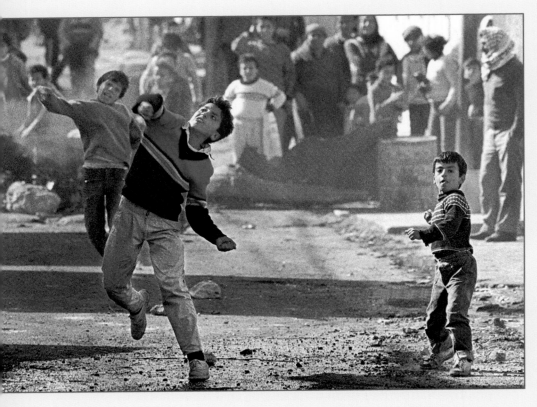

Tired of being forced to live under Israeli occupation forces, Palestinians took action by organizing boycotts, demonstrations, and strikes during the first intifada. Children were encouraged to throw rocks at Israeli soldiers, acts that resulted in dangerous skirmishes and even deaths.

As the intifada raged on, Israelis searched for viable, non-military solutions to the seemingly endless cycle of violence that had developed between their nation and the Palestinians of the occupied territories. Many believed that opening a dialogue with the PLO was a necessary first step to attaining peace, despite the persistent refusal of Israel's leadership, Labor and Likud alike, to negotiate with what they had dismissed as a terrorist group since the PLO's founding in 1964.

THE ROAD TO NEGOTIATIONS

By the early 1990s, dealing with the PLO seemed more vital than ever to Israelis seeking a diplomatic resolution to the escalating Palestinian conflict. Although the intifada had begun as a grassroots movement and was not instigated by the PLO, the organization's representatives soon emerged as the uprising's acknowledged leaders and spokespersons. Further strengthening the PLO's claim to speak for the Palestinians of the occupied territories was the decision of Jordan, which had governed the West Bank from 1949 to the War of 1967, to formally renounce all claims to the region in 1988 in favor of the PLO.

Meanwhile, as many Israelis were becoming convinced that negotiating with the PLO was their best hope for securing a peaceful end to the intifada, world events were moving the PLO toward a more conciliatory stance regarding the Jewish state. During the Gulf War of 1991, Arafat and the PLO made the grave mistake of supporting Iraqi President Saddam Hussein, a strident critic of Israel. This put Arafat and his organization at odds with two of the PLO's most generous financial supporters in the past: Kuwait, which Hussein invaded and plundered in 1990, and Saudi Arabia, which joined with the United States and a coalition of other Western and Arab nations to expel Iraq from Kuwait in the Gulf War of 1991. In the wake of the Gulf War, the two oil-rich Gulf states shunned the PLO, cutting the organization off from what had long been a central source of its funding. Israel, in contrast, consolidated its U.S. support during the war by agreeing to follow U.S. President George H. W. Bush's appeal for restraint in the face of Iraqi air attacks on the country. During the course of the conflict, Iraq fired 40 Scud ballistic missiles into Tel Aviv and Haifa. Although few injuries or deaths resulted from the attacks, Israelis were outraged. Nonetheless, when the Bush administration, anxious to keep its Middle Eastern coalition together, urged Israel not to retaliate, Israel complied, albeit reluctantly.

Adding to the PLO's troubles was the disintegration of the Soviet Union that same year. Since the 1950s the Soviet Union had consistently backed the Arab powers in their military conflicts with Israel as part of their fierce Cold War rivalry with the United States, Israel's chief ally. Thus, with the official collapse of the Soviet Union in 1991 and the end of the Cold War, an important potential source of military and financial aid for the Palestinians in their struggle against the Jewish state vanished.

Finally, in addition to external events like the Gulf War and the fall of the Soviet Union, there were also internal factors pushing the PLO leadership toward negotiations with their old enemy. The Israeli government used the Gulf War as an excuse to crack down more harshly than ever on the intifada. During the war, the Palestinian populations of the Gaza Strip and West Bank were placed under an almost total curfew and deportations from the occupied territories of those Arabs deemed as troublemakers by Israeli officials multiplied. The curfew, combined with a temporary prohibition on Palestinian laborers entering Israel from the territories to work, all but crippled the Palestinian economy in Gaza and the West Bank. There was a growing feeling among many Palestinians that the time had come to relinquish old dreams of reclaiming all of Palestine from the Jews in favor of creating a separate Palestinian state alongside Israel in the West Bank and Gaza. As the intifada dragged on with no end in sight, they put increasing pressure on Arafat and other PLO leaders to take concrete steps toward realizing that goal.

THE PEACE PROCESS TAKES SHAPE

In the national elections of 1992, the Israeli people demonstrated their readiness to open negotiations with the Palestinians and their PLO representatives through their overwhelming support of the Labor Party and its leader, Yitzhak Rabin, a champion of the peace process. The first native-born prime minister of Israel, Rabin was also a much-admired national hero. As the chief of

After the Gulf War in 1991, President George H.W. Bush *(middle)* arrived with Israeli prime minister Yitzhak Rabin *(foreground)* and his wife Leah Rabin *(background)* in Madrid, Spain, to begin peace talks with Palestinian representatives. Israel's first native-born prime minister, as well as its youngest, Rabin was able to forge relationships that would lead to peace in northern Israel and the adoption of the Oslo Accords between his country and the Palestinians.

staff of the IDF, he had helped lead his country to victory in the Six-Day War of 1967. Rabin and his Labor cohorts replaced a right-wing government headed by Shamir, which had assumed power two years earlier when the national unity government formed in 1988 disintegrated over the issue of initiating talks with the Palestinians. Contributing to Labor's 1992 win was a massive bloc of voters who had recently emigrated from the former Soviet Union. These new Jewish immigrants, having lived all their lives under the Soviet Union's communist system, had little sympathy for the Likud's right-wing economic policies, preferring the moderate socialism of the Labor Party.

Immediately following the Gulf War in 1991, the administration of U.S. President George H.W. Bush had helped arrange peace talks in Madrid, Spain, between Israel and its Arab neighbors. Bush was eager to maintain the anti-Iraq coalition of Arab states his administration had created during the war and worried that the continued lack of an Israeli-Arab peace would endanger that fragile alliance. Although Palestinian representatives with ties to the PLO had been present at the talks, the PLO leadership was officially excluded, and the talks proved largely unproductive. Labor's victory in 1992 convinced Rabin that the majority of Israelis supported a wider commitment to the peace process, including a willingness to deal with Chairman Arafat and other PLO leaders.

In early 1993, therefore, the new Israeli government lifted the nation's nearly three decade–long ban on contacts with the PLO. Following months of secret Israeli-PLO negotiations in Oslo, Norway, Rabin and Arafat announced they had achieved a breakthrough. In the so-called Oslo Accords of September 1993, the PLO consented to recognize Israel's right to exist and to renounce violence against the Jewish state in return for Israel's recognition and its phased withdrawal from predominantly Arab areas in the Gaza Strip and West Bank. An interim, confidence-building period of five years, during which Israeli troops would gradually pull out of Arab sectors in the territories and the Palestinians in those areas would attain limited self-rule, was agreed to by both parties. The most explosive and painful issues dividing the Israelis and Palestinians, including the status of East Jerusalem and the Old City (claimed by both sides), the future of well over 100 Jewish settlements scattered throughout the occupied territories, and the right of several million Palestinian refugees from the Arab-Israeli War of 1948 to return to Israel, were to be deferred until the end of the interim period.

Further negotiations between the PLO and Israel in 1994 and 1995 resulted in Palestinians taking control over education, taxation, criminal justice, health care, and other civil functions in the Gaza Strip and in most Arab population centers in the West Bank under the direction of a new political body, the Palestinian Authority (PA). In 1996, PLO Chairman Yasir Arafat was elected as the head of the PA. Israel pledged to carry out troop withdrawals from additional Arab towns and villages in the West Bank following the PA elections, after which negotiations regarding the ultimate status of the Palestinian areas would commence.

With the Palestinians and Israelis apparently moving toward a peaceful resolution of their long conflict, some Arab nations approached Israel regarding the normalization of relations. Although peace negotiations between Israel and its neighbors Lebanon and Syria failed, Israel secured diplomatic ties with several Arab nations in the Persian Gulf and North Africa. In 1994, the Israeli government signed a historic peace treaty with Jordan. Jordan's King Hussein, although censured by many of his fellow Arabs for placing peace with Israel above loyalty to the Palestinians, was determined to finally end the nearly half century of belligerence between his country and its neighbor to the west.

A FALTERING PEACE PROCESS

Not all Israelis supported the Oslo peace process. Some Israelis, and especially religious nationalists who viewed the West Bank (or Judea and Samaria, as they called it) as part of "Greater Israel" and the Jewish people's rightful inheritance, were bitterly opposed to permitting Palestinian self-rule in the territories. Many also worried that further peace agreements with the Palestinians would entail the dismantling of Jewish settlements in the West Bank, an action they strongly disapproved. Some of the most strident critics of the peace process even went so far as to brand Prime Minister Rabin as a "traitor" and an "oppressor" of his own people. On the evening of November 4, 1995, an Israeli university student and religious extremist who condemned the peace process as treasonous shot and killed Rabin as he left a peace rally in Tel Aviv. In a speech before tens of thousands of peace supporters just moments earlier, Rabin had said: "I have always believed that the majority of the people want peace, are prepared to take risks for peace. And you here, by showing up at this rally, prove it, along with the many who did not make it here, that the people truly want peace and oppose violence."

After Rabin's death, his successor and close friend, Shimon Peres, pledged to carry on the peace program begun in Oslo. At his funeral, Rabin was eulogized by Egyptian President Hosni Mubarak, King Hussein of Jordan, and Prime Minister Peres, among others. " I see our people in profound shock, with tears in their eyes, but also a people who know that the bullets that murdered you could not murder the idea which you embraced," said Peres. "You did not leave us a last will, but you left us a path on which we will march with conviction and faith. . . . I see our Arab neighbors and to them I say: The course of peace is irreversible. Neither for us, nor for you. Neither we nor you can stop, delay or hesitate when it comes to peace—a peace that must be full and comprehensive, for young and old, for all the peoples."

Unfortunately for Peres and other advocates of the peace process, however, two growing groups of Palestinian-Islamic militants, Hamas and Islamic Jihad, were as determined to derail the peace negotiations as Rabin's young Jewish assassin had been. The PLO had traditionally emphasized secular nationalism. (*Secular* means "concerned with nonreligious things.") Founded by Islamic fundamentalists in the Gaza Strip in 1981 and 1987, respectively, the Islamic Jihad and Hamas linked the religion of Islam closely to the Palestinian cause, claiming that Israel was a source of spiritual corruption for Muslims and must be destroyed and replaced with a Palestinian Islamic state. The larger of the two groups, Hamas, quickly developed into a mass movement in the West Bank and Gaza with an extensive network of charitable and religious institutions and an active political wing. The existing peace process, both Hamas and Islamic Jihad believed, amounted to a PLO sellout of Palestine. All of the Jewish state belonged to the Islamic Palestinians, from the Jordan River all the way to the Mediterranean Sea, they contended, and Palestinians should not settle for anything less than their entire homeland.

In hopes of subverting the peace process, Hamas and Islamic Jihad terrorists launched a wave of devastating suicide bombings in Israeli cities in 1995 and 1996. By the time of the national elections in the spring of 1996, the atmosphere of fear and uncertainty generated by the terrorists had pushed many voters into the Likud camp, now led by Binyamin Netanyahu, an outspoken critic of the peace program initiated by Rabin. Claiming that the peace process undermined the safety of the Israeli people, Netanyahu campaigned under the slogan: "There is no peace. There is no security. There is no reason to vote for Peres." In May 1996, Netanyahu defeated Labor's Peres in Israel's first direct elections for prime minister by a razor-slim margin.

With Netanyahu in office, the peace process immediately began to founder. The new prime minister angered the Palestinians by ending a Labor Party freeze on constructing new Jewish settlements in East Jerusalem, an action Palestinian leaders blasted as an indication of bad faith. Netanyahu further inflamed Palestinian opinion by opening a tunnel for archaeological excavation near one of the Islamic religion's holiest sites, the Al Aqsa Mosque on the Temple Mount in Jerusalem's Old City (also the site of the Western Wall).

Despite his outspoken opposition to the existing peace process, under strong internal and international pressure—

particularly from the United States—Netanyahu resumed talks with Arafat, and in 1997 transferred 80 percent of the predominantly Arab town of Hebron in the West Bank to the PA. The following year, he signed the Wye River Memorandum at peace talks sponsored by U.S. President Bill Clinton. The Wye River Memorandum tied Israeli withdrawal from an additional 13 percent of the West Bank to security guarantees from the PA against terrorist attacks on Israelis. Upon completion of the Wye withdrawal process, the vast majority of the Palestinian population in the West Bank and about 40 percent of the West Bank's territory would be under PA control. Phased implementation of the agreement was to be followed by the final talks on the status of the West Bank and Gaza arranged for in the Oslo Accords of 1993.

Netanyahu's government, however, never carried through with the terms outlined in the Wye River Memorandum. The strong opposition to the agreement among hard-line members of his rightist coalition led Netanyahu to halt the transfer of the West Bank territory outlined in the document after some nine percent of the land had been handed over to the PA. Growing public frustration in Israel over the stalled peace process resulted in the landslide election of Labor's Ehud Barak as prime minister in 1999. Barak, a highly decorated former general in the IDF, pledged in his campaign to adhere to the terms of the Wye River agreement and get the peace process back on track.

THE CAMP DAVID SUMMIT
AND A SECOND INTIFADA

During the summer of 2000, Bill Clinton, seeking to move the Palestinian-Israeli peace process forward, brought Barak and Arafat together for negotiating sessions at his presidential retreat in Camp David. Determined to finalize the peace process once and for all, Barak arrived at Camp David ready to make concessions. He offered Arafat partial control of Jerusalem's Old City, Israeli withdrawal from more than 90 percent of the West Bank and virtually the entire Gaza Strip, and the dismantling of many—but not all—Jewish settlements in both areas. In exchange, he wanted a formal Palestinian renunciation of all demands for a return to Israel.

Although Barak and many other Israelis viewed his offers as generous, Arafat spurned them, declaring that a "right of return" to Israel for all Palestinian refugees of the Arab-Israeli War of 1948 and their descendants was central to any final peace agreement between Israel and the Palestinians. This was going too far for Barak, who balked at allowing some 3.5 million refugees living in refugee camps in the West Bank and Gaza as well as in Lebanon, Syria, Jordan, and other Arab nations into Israel, a course of action that he, like most of his compatriots, believed would mean the demise of Israel as a Jewish state. Instead, Barak proposed either letting those refugees in other Arab states return to a new Palestinian state created from the former occupied territories or having them stay where they were and receive financial compensation from the international community. Barak undoubtedly hoped that those who stayed put would also secure full citizenship from their countries of residence, something most Palestinian refugees have been denied through the years by their Arab host governments, with the exception of Jordan.

Arafat rebuffed Barak's new offers regarding the Palestinian exiles as well. In addition to the refugee issue, the question of Jerusalem, and particularly of which group should control the holy places in the walled Old City between West and East Jerusalem, was another sticking point for the PA head. Although Barak was prepared to relinquish East Jerusalem to the Palestinians to serve as their new state's capital, Arafat accused Barak of not allowing the Palestinians enough say over the Old City. He was particularly concerned about the Al Aqsa Mosque and another nearby mosque called the Dome of the Rock, whose grounds double as the Jewish temple Mount, the site of the Western Wall and the ancient temples destroyed by the Babylonians and the Romans. A few months after the Camp David Summit, a second round of peace talks in Taba, Egypt, in which Barak promised Arafat additional West Bank territory and more control

Likud leader Ariel Sharon *(above)* sparked riots when he visited the Temple Mount, one of the holiest sites in both Judaism and Islam. Part of the territory that was seized by Israeli forces in 1967, the Temple Mount encompasses the Wailing Wall, a revered Jewish relic, and the Dome of the Rock, an important Islamic shrine. Politicians on both sides accused Sharon of inflaming an already excitable public with his controversial action.

over the Temple Mount/Al Aqsa Mosque complex, also ended in stalemate.

Arafat and Barak's inability to finalize the peace process produced deep frustration among Israelis and Palestinians alike. In the atmosphere of mistrust surrounding the diplomatic stalemate, Ariel Sharon, the new Likud leader, toured the Temple Mount in September 2000. Sharon's highly publicized visit to the sacred grounds was seen by many Palestinians as being deliberately provocative in light of the long-standing dispute between Muslims and Jews over their religions' Old City shrines.

In the wake of Sharon's controversial tour, bloody Palestinian riots erupted at the Al Aqsa Mosque, then rapidly spread throughout the West Bank and Gaza. In an effort to end the violence, the United States convened a peace summit in Sharm-El Sheikh, Egypt, on October 17–18. Both the Israeli and Palestinian delegates pledged to return to the negotiating table and issue public statements denouncing the violence. Nonetheless, just three days after the Sharm-El Sheikh summit, Arafat and other Arab leaders, meeting at an emergency summit of the Arab League in Cairo, Egypt, published a formal statement strongly endorsing the new intifada in the occupied territories and the "valiant" Palestinians who had instigated it. Soon after, a car bombing in an outdoor market in Jerusalem by a member of the Islamic Jihad killed two and wounded 10 Israelis, making it quite clear that the Al Aqsa Intifada was far from over.

8

Into the Twenty-First Century: The Challenge Continues

The second intifada (known to Palestinians as the Al Aqsa Intifada), was far more deadly than the first. It featured recurrent shootings by Palestinian militias and suicide bombings in Israeli shopping malls, cafés, grocery stores, and other heavily frequented places by Hamas and Islamic Jihad terrorists, and eventually by a group associated with the PLO, the Al Aqsa Martyrs Brigade.

ARIEL SHARON TAKES CHARGE

The IDF responded to the escalating violence by imposing restrictions on West Bank and Gaza Palestinians, including curfews, heavily policed checkpoints, and blockades. Still the guerrilla attacks and suicide bombings continued. In February 2001, national elections resulted in a landslide victory for the Likud's hawkish Ariel Sharon as disillusioned and fearful Israelis repudiated the peace process begun nearly a decade earlier in favor of Sharon's call for a tougher approach to the Palestinian unrest.

Under Sharon's rule, the death toll climbed as Israeli forces assassinated Palestinian militants and carried out incursions into PA areas, while Palestinians, in turn, escalated their attacks on Israeli civilians and soldiers. Sharon refused to negotiate with PA head Arafat as long as the Palestinian violence persisted. Arafat declared cease-fires several times during 2001, including in June when the murder of 21 Israeli teenagers at a Tel Aviv dance club by a Palestinian suicide bomber drew widespread international condemnation, and following the attacks on the World Trade Center and the Pentagon in the United States by the Islamic terrorist group, al Qaeda, on September 11. None of the cease-fires held for long, however, and in October 2001 Sharon placed Arafat under virtual house arrest in his West Bank head-quarters at Ramallah following the assassination of a right-wing cabinet minister by Palestinian militants. Arafat would not be released until April 28, 2002, following a month-long siege on Ramallah by Israeli forces.

Meanwhile, at a summit held in Beirut in March 2002, the Arab League formally endorsed a Palestinian-Israeli peace plan generated by the Saudi Arabian government. The Saudi proposal offered Israel full diplomatic and economic relations with the Arab states in exchange for its withdrawal to pre–June 1967 borders and the creation of a Palestinian state encompassing all the West Bank and the Gaza Strip. Declaring that a return to the 1967 borders was unacceptable because it would jeopardize national security, Sharon nonetheless expressed a willingness to engage in regional Middle East peace talks—assuming those talks did not include Arafat, whom Sharon dismissed as an unrepentant terrorist. Given Sharon's longtime commitment to Jewish settlement in the West Bank, it seems likely his objection to the Saudi peace scheme was also influenced by the fact that the plan would entail the dismantling of all Israeli settlements there (currently inhabited by nearly 200,000 Jews).

After a spate of bloody suicide attacks and car bombings in Israeli cities, while the Arab League was still meeting in Beirut to discuss a Middle East peace plan, Palestinian terrorists carried out their most deadly suicide bombing to date. On the evening of March 27, in the seaside resort of Netanya, a member of the militant Hamas organization strapped powerful explosives to his body and blew himself up in a hotel restaurant filled with

Jewish families celebrating the Passover holiday. Twenty-nine people, including a number of elderly Holocaust survivors, were killed and 150 wounded in the assault. As a furious Sharon vowed to destroy the terrorist "infrastructure," Israeli tanks rolled into West Bank refugee camps and cities, arresting suspected terrorists, destroying bomb factories as well as a number of homes and other buildings, and confiscating huge caches of weapons in Israel's biggest military action since the war in Lebanon.

As part of Operation Defensive Shield, the Israeli government's name for the massive counterterrorist offensive, in early April 2002 IDF tanks and troops invaded the crowded West Bank refugee camp of Jenin. Controlled by the Palestinian Authority since 1995, Jenin had become a breeding ground for terrorism during the second intifada. The camp had turned out nearly 30 suicide bombers, including the Netanya bomber, and housed numerous explosive-making labs. For more than a week, the IDF battled with heavily armed terrorist groups in Jenin. After finally gaining control of the camp, the Israelis announced that 23 IDF soldiers and 52 Palestinians had died in the fighting, most of them members of the terrorist organizations Hamas, Islamic Jihad, and the Al Aqsa Martyrs Brigade. Some Palestinians, however, accused the IDF of carrying out a cold-blooded massacre in Jenin. Their charges that the IDF had slaughtered dozens of innocent civilians at Jenin were quickly picked up by the world press and prompted investigations by the United Nations and the private international organization Human Rights Watch. Both investigations supported Israeli reports that 52 Palestinians—mostly armed militants—were killed in Jenin in April 2002. Nonetheless, Human Rights Watch criticized the IDF for preventing humanitarian organizations from accessing the camp for several days after the battle.

After the controversial Israeli invasion of Jenin, U.S. President George W. Bush sent his secretary of state, Colin Powell, to the Middle East to broker a cease-fire between the Palestinians and Israelis and to try to halt attacks on Israel's northern border by the militant Islamic group, Hizbollah. Both Iran and Syria sponsor Hizbollah, which operates out of bases in southern Lebanon and calls for the complete destruction of the Jewish state. The Bush administration's desire to calm the escalating Israeli-Palestinian dispute was at least partly motivated by its need to build a strong Middle Eastern alliance against Iraq. Ever since the terrorist attacks in September 11, 2001, in New York City and Washington, D.C., Bush had been publicly calling for a change of regime in Iraq. Since 1979 the oil-rich nation had been led by Saddam Hussein, whom the Bush administration accused of secretly developing weapons of mass destruction and aiding and abetting terrorists. Powell's peace mission came to nothing, however. Sharon adamantly refused Powell's entreaties to withdraw IDF troops from the West Bank areas they had reoccupied during Operation Defensive Shield; nor could the U.S. secretary of state talk the Palestinians into proclaiming a truce.

On their incursions into Palestinian Authority–governed areas as part of Operation Defensive Shield, the IDF had captured a number of documents showing that, despite his public condemnations of terrorism in recent years, Yasir Arafat was personally involved in setting up and funding terror cells. In the wake of these revelations, the U.S. and Israeli governments increasingly viewed Arafat as a chief architect of the Palestinian terror campaign and a major stumbling block to peace. Consequently, in June 2002 President Bush called on Palestinians to oust Arafat as head of the Palestinian Authority and vote in new leaders who "were not compromised by terror." Soon after, diplomats from the United States, the European Union, Russia, and the United Nations—the so-called Quartet—formally endorsed the Bush administration's "Road Map for Peace in the Middle East." The Road Map plan for a Palestinian-Israeli peace settlement by 2005 called for Israeli withdrawal from the Palestinian areas it reoccupied in the spring of 2002 during Operation Defensive Shield, a freeze on Israeli settlement in the West Bank and Gaza, and the creation of an independent Palestinian state. In their turn, Palestinian officials were to oversee the disbanding of terrorist factions and the reform of the authoritarian Palestinian Authority government to make it more democratic.

As the summer of 2002 progressed, however, it began to seem more and more unlikely that Israeli withdrawal from the occupied territories would happen anytime soon. In response to a new wave of Palestinian suicide attacks, in June, Sharon

Palestinian leader and revolutionary Yasir Arafat waves to the crowd in Jenin, a town in the West Bank, one last time before his confinement in Ramallah. Israeli government officials, claiming that Arafat had not done enough to track down militants and suicide bombers, surrounded his headquarters with snipers and tanks. Arafat was granted a release later only on medical grounds.

had launched a massive new counterterrorism offensive in the West Bank dubbed Operation Determined Path. After a particularly bloody suicide bombing of a crowded Tel Aviv bus in mid-September, the IDF once again besieged Arafat's West Bank headquarters at Ramallah, demolishing much of the complex and cutting off Arafat's building from the rest of the compound. After 11 days, Israel finally pulled its tanks out of Ramallah in response to intense pressure from the Bush administration, which feared that the siege was undermining its efforts to secure Arab support for their upcoming attack on Iraq. Nonetheless, within a few days Israeli troops had reoccupied several buildings close to Arafat's headquarters, and for the next three years Israeli forces would keep the Palestinian leader under virtual house arrest in Ramallah.

WAR IN IRAQ AND RENEWED HOPES FOR PEACE

Early on the morning of March 20, 2003, despite widespread opposition from within and outside the United States, U.S.–led coalition forces launched a long-anticipated invasion of Iraq to overthrow the regime of Saddam Hussein. By early April, U.S. forces had taken control of Baghdad, Iraq's capital city. On May 1, 2003, President Bush declared the war officially over. In reality, the rise of a powerful insurgent movement and bitter ethnic and religious rivalries would keep the country mired in violence and political turmoil for years to come.

The swiftness of Saddam's defeat by the U.S.–led forces in the spring of 2003 made a deep impression on the Palestinian leadership. Palestinians had long maintained a friendly relationship with the Iraqi dictator, who had launched several dozen Scud ballistic missiles into Israeli cities during the Gulf War of 1991. Shortly before the invasion of March 2003, Saddam had presented a total of $260,000 to 26 families of Palestinians who had been killed during the second intifada. In common with many of their Arab neighbors, the Palestinians publicly criticized the U.S. occupation of Iraq following Baghdad's fall.

Nonetheless, in the wake of the successful invasion, Palestinian leaders also stressed their willingness to institute democratic reforms in the PA, something the architects of the Road Map for Peace, and particularly the United States, had been pressing hard for over the course of the last year.

On April 29, Mahmoud Abbas, a longtime PLO member whom the United States and Israel both viewed as more moderate and amenable to compromise than Arafat, was formally elected by the Palestinian parliament as the PA's first prime minister. His election meant that President Arafat would now be compelled to share power over the Palestinian Authority with Abbas and a cabinet appointed by the new prime minister. Encouraged by this significant step toward democratic reform, on April 30 representatives of the Quartet formally presented Abbas with a copy of the Road Map for Peace, which the new prime minister and his cabinet promptly approved.

On May 25, the Israeli government also officially approved the Road Map for Peace. Heartened by the election of the moderate Abbas and anxious to retain vital American economic and military support for Israel, Sharon had convinced his cabinet to accept the plan despite strong right-wing objections. Since taking power in 2001, Sharon had stubbornly refused to meet with Arafat because of the Palestinian leader's links to terrorism, but on May 29, 2003, Sharon invited Prime Minister Abbas to visit him in Jerusalem. Several days later at a high-profile summit held in Al-'Aqabah, Jordan, Sharon and Abbas, in the presence of President Bush, pledged to meet the conditions of the Road Map and shook hands.

Yet renewed hopes for peace in the wake of Abbas's election were to prove illusory. The Road Map for Peace required the PA to immediately disband Palestinian terrorist groups and confiscate their weapons. Abbas, however, insisted that disarming the militants before Israel began any meaningful withdrawal of troops from Gaza and the West Bank would cause widespread anger and distrust and possibly even spark a civil war pitting Hamas and other terrorist groups against the PA government.

Sharon, in turn, refused to vacate Palestinian trouble spots in Gaza and the West Bank until he saw clear evidence that Abbas was reining in the terrorists. After a short break from the usual cycle of terrorist violence and Israeli retaliatory raids against Palestinian targets, on August 20 a Hamas suicide bombing killed 21 people on a Jerusalem bus; the next day Israel assassinated the organization's top leader. On September 6, 2003, after just 100 days in office, Abbas, frustrated both by Sharon's intransigence and Arafat's ongoing efforts to control him and his cabinet, resigned as prime minister. In his stead, Ahmed Qurei, a loyal supporter of Arafat, was appointed.

On November 11, 2004, a little more than a year after Qurei's appointment, Arafat, the president of the Palestinian Authority since its creation in 1994 and the leader of the PLO for four decades, died in a Parisian hospital at the age of 75. In January 2005, the moderate Mahmoud Abbas was elected as president of the PA, a promising development that revived hopes for a peaceful settlement in Israel and much of the international community.

DISENGAGEMENT FROM GAZA AND A CONTROVERSIAL SECURITY BARRIER

Several months before Arafat's death, the hawkish Sharon had surprised the world by announcing his plan to withdraw Israeli troops and nearly 8,000 Israeli settlers from the Gaza Strip and a handful of settlements in the northern West Bank by mid-2005. Although the Palestinian government immediately lauded Sharon's disengagement plan, it was loudly censured by the prime minister's own party, the right-wing Likud. Nonetheless, shortly after a summit at Sharm-El Sheikh, Egypt, in February 2005 at which both Sharon and the newly elected President Abbas declared an informal truce, Sharon was able to win the Knesset's approval for his disengagement scheme. Despite widespread and angry protests by settlers, removal of all Israeli troops and settlers from Gaza was completed by September of that year, nearly

40 years after Israel had first captured the Gaza Strip during the Six-Day War. Two months later, fed up with continued criticism of his leadership by his colleagues in the Likud Party, Sharon broke with his longtime political party to form a new centrist party called the Kadima Party.

As Sharon was withdrawing Israeli troops and settlers from Gaza, he was also moving ahead with a controversial project involving the West Bank begun by his predecessor, Ehud Barak: the West Bank security barrier. From June 2002, when construction on the structure started, the 480-mile barrier had been a major area of contention between the Palestinian Authority and the Israeli government. According to Israeli officials, the sole purpose of the barrier, which is a fence along most of its length but consists of high concrete walls in several especially vulnerable areas, was to prevent suicide bombers from infiltrating Israel proper from the West Bank. Many Palestinians, however, believed that what the Israeli government was really after was an illegal land grab. They were outraged when they discovered that major segments of the barrier were to be constructed not on Israeli land but on Palestinian land, and that it would enclose several populous Israeli settlements within the West Bank, including East Jerusalem and Ariel. The United Nations, as well as a number of human rights organizations and Israeli peace groups, also objected to the barrier, noting that it virtually sealed off several Palestinian towns and divided many other villagers from their farm fields, water sources, or workplaces.

In late 2003, as Sharon's administration pushed ahead with construction of the controversial barrier, the UN General Assembly adopted a resolution requesting the International Court of Justice at the Hague to review its legality. Six months later, on July 9, 2004, the Court of Justice ruled that the barrier violated human rights and must be removed. Israel refused to accept the court's decision but announced it would modify the barrier's route in line with the rulings of the Israeli Supreme Court. In 2005, after the Supreme Court ruled that the original path was unnecessarily disruptive to the lives of West Bank Palestinians,

Built to prevent Arab militants from attacking Israeli citizens, the West Bank security barrier caused a local and international uproar. The Israeli government adjusted certain parts of the barrier after the United Nations and Palestinians objected to its construction. It is estimated that the structure costs $2 million per kilometer.

the barrier was rerouted closer to the so-called Green Line—Israel's boundary with the West Bank immediately following the first Arab-Israeli War of 1948–1949. In 2006, the route was changed again to leave less West Bank land—about five percent in all—on the western, Israeli side of the security fence. Today a majority of Israelis support the barrier, viewing it is a critical factor in the dramatic reduction of terrorist acts within Israel proper by more than 90 percent from 2002 until 2006.

THE RISE OF HAMAS AND CONFLICTS IN GAZA AND LEBANON

Both the Israeli and the Palestinian governments experienced major and unexpected changes during the first month of 2006. First, on January 4, Israel's longtime leader, Ariel Sharon, suffered an incapacitating stroke and Deputy Prime Minister Ehud Olmert, a fellow Kadima member, took over the reins of government as acting prime minister. Just three weeks later, on January 25, the government of the Palestinian Authority also underwent a dramatic transformation when national elections gave the political wing of Hamas a majority of seats in the Palestinian Legislative Council. Hamas's victory came at the expense of the PLO's political wing, Fatah, the party of President Abbas and the late Yasir Arafat and the dominant force in the PA's governing body since 1994. By the early twenty-first century, Hamas was far and away the largest and most powerful of the various militant Islamic Palestinian organizations that had developed in the 1980s. The group's popularity among the Palestinian people was directly linked to its generous support for much-needed social programs in Gaza and the West Bank, including the building of hospitals and schools. Nonetheless, the victory in the January 2006 elections of an organization so closely tied to terrorism, including numerous horrific suicide bombings in Jerusalem, Tel Aviv, and other cities over the past six years, deeply dismayed Israel and much of the rest of the world.

In the wake of Hamas's legislative victory, the Israeli government froze all relations with the Palestinian Authority. U.S. and European leaders also vowed not to have any dealings with Hamas until they agreed to disarm, recognize the right of the State of Israel to exist, and honor previous Palestinian-Israeli agreements. Hamas spokesmen promptly rejected all three conditions. They did, however, try to negotiate the formation of a national unity government with the more moderate Fatah party in hopes of convincing the United States and European Union to resume the financial aid to the PA that most of the Western powers had suspended following the January election. Yet efforts to reach a compromise between Hamas and President Abbas and his Fatah party over the next few months proved fruitless. When Abbas declared a new Hamas security militia to be illegal and formed a rival Fatah-based militia, fighting between Fatah and Hamas militiamen erupted in Gaza and numerous officials from both organizations were abducted or assassinated.

While Hamas and Fatah were engaged in an increasingly violent struggle for supremacy in Gaza, the ongoing conflict between Hamas and Israel was also escalating. Soon after IDF forces withdrew from the Gaza Strip during the summer of 2005, Hamas terrorists had begun firing crude rockets into northern Israeli towns from Gaza. On June 25, 2006, they slipped into Israel and launched a bold raid on an IDF border post that resulted in the death of two Israeli soldiers and the kidnapping of a third. Israel immediately retaliated with Operation Summer Rains, a major military invasion designed to pressure Hamas into returning the kidnapped soldier alive and stopping the rain of rockets on Israeli communities from Gaza launching sites. In a series of cross-border raids, the IDF destroyed rocket launching sites and stockpiles and arrested and killed hundreds of Hamas militants.

In July 2006, the IDF found itself embroiled in yet another border conflict, this time involving Hizbollah militants in southern Lebanon. On July 12, Hizbollah fighters attacked an IDF patrol in northern Israel, eventually killing eight soldiers and kidnapping two others. At the same time, Hizbollah initiated a series of destructive rocket assaults on Haifa, Safed, and other towns and cities well within northern Israel. In response to Hizbollah's stepped-up campaign of terror against Israel, Prime Minister Olmert approved another major military campaign—Operation Just Reward. Massive air strikes against

Classified as a terrorist organization by the United States, the United Nations, and the European Union, Hamas managed to win power in the Palestinian parliament in January 2006. A group famous for its suicide bombings and assassinations, Hamas has amassed large numbers of supporters *(above)* by building schools and hospitals and maintaining popular social programs.

rocket launchers in southern Lebanon and Hizbollah rocket stockpiles and headquarters in Beirut resulted in hundreds of casualties, many of them Lebanese civilians. The Hizbollah-Israeli conflict finally ended on August 14 following the passage of UN Security Council Resolution 1701. The resolution called for an immediate cease-fire, an embargo on all weapons sales to Hizbollah, and the deployment in Southern Lebanon of the Lebanese army backed by a multinational UN peace-keeping force to recapture control of the region from Hizbollah militants. The kidnapped IDF soldiers were not returned, however. In November 2006, Israelis and Palestinians agreed to a cease-fire in the ongoing Gaza conflict, although sporadic rocket attacks from Hamas militants on Israeli border towns continued.

In early February 2006, Fatah and Hamas finally reached a power-sharing agreement and announced the formation of a new national unity government. Abbas was once again appointed president and was to be assisted by two prime ministers: Fatah member Ahmad Qurei and, from March 29 on, Hamas member Ismail Haniya. Although the unity agreement did not include Palestinian recognition of Israel or a commitment to disarm militant factions, the United States and other Western powers were hopeful that the new coalition government would adopt a more moderate stance toward Israel. The following month, the Arab League Summit in Riyadh, Saudi Arabia, reiterated the league's support for the Palestinian-Israeli peace plan first proposed by the Saudis in March 2002. In response Ehud Olmert expressed Israel's interest in using the Arab peace initiative as a starting point for negotiations with the Palestinians.

ISRAEL'S UNCERTAIN FUTURE

During the summer of 2007, the fragile truce between the radical Hamas and the more moderate Fatah party disintegrated in the Gaza Strip. To the consternation of Israel and most of the Western world, in June Hamas paramilitary forces managed to kill or exile all senior Fatah officials in Gaza and take sole charge of the strip and its population of 1.4 million Palestinians.

Although a major setback for the Israeli-Palestinian peace process, the takeover of Gaza by the virulently anti-Israel Hamas faction has not completely derailed it. Shortly after the Hamas victory in June, President Abbas angrily dissolved the Hamas-led Palestinian government in the West Bank and appointed his own emergency cabinet. In response to this welcome move by Fatah's top leader, Prime Minister Olmert freed more than 250 Fatah prisoners from Israeli jails. He also pledged to improve living conditions for the West Bank's approximately 2.5 million Palestinian inhabitants and schedule regular talks with Abbas regarding Palestinian statehood.

While Olmert's recent actions are certainly encouraging, the Israeli-Palestinian peace process still faces formidable stumbling blocks. Most important are the fundamentally conflicting goals of the Palestinian and Israeli governments. Both sides agree that they want a fully independent Palestinian state. Yet the new Palestinian state envisioned by Olmert would exclude most of the Jewish settlements in east Jerusalem and the West Bank, while the state envisioned by Abbas would encompass all of Jerusalem and the other West Bank territories occupied by Israel in 1967. In March 2008, Olmert angered Abbas and other Fatah leaders by announcing that Israel would continue to build in those parts of Jerusalem and the West Bank that it wants to retain in a future peace deal. The longstanding Palestinian demand for the right of return of Palestinian refugees to Israel proper is another crucial sticking point between Abbas and Olmert. Like most Israelis, Olmert fears that allowing large numbers of Palestinians to settle in Israel would inevitably destroy the Jewish nature of the state.

In the early twenty-first century, Israel is the most economically, technically, and militarily advanced nation in the Middle East. Yet six decades after the creation of the modern Israeli nation, the Zionist dream of an enduring Jewish state in the biblical Promised Land still does not appear assured. Powerful Islamic militant organizations in the West Bank and particularly in Hamas-controlled Gaza, and recent arms buildups by Hizbollah forces in southern Lebanon and by Syria, which still deeply resents Israel's annexation of the Golan Heights, pose grave threats to Israeli lives and property. A potentially even greater danger to the small state comes from a nation that does not share a border with it—Iran. Under the leadership of its venomously anti-Israeli president, Mahmoud Ahmadinejad, Iran has declared the annihilation of the Jewish state as a foreign policy priority and has reputedly served as a major arms supplier for Hizbollah and Hamas. Of even greater concern to Israel are Iran's alleged nuclear ambitions. Both the United States and the Israeli governments have repeated accused Iran of trying to develop its own nuclear bombs, weapons capable of giving substance to Ahmadinejad's sensationalist rhetoric regarding Israel, which he has characterized as "a disgraceful blot" that "must be wiped off the map of the world."

From the nation's beginnings in May 1948 until the present day, the central fact of Israel's existence has been its ongoing fight for survival within a hostile environment. As Israel's second half century of statehood unfolds, it can only be hoped the embattled country will at last find a way to live in peace with the Palestinians and with all of its neighbors in the Middle East.

Chronology

B.C.

c. 1800   Hebrews settle in Canaan.

1020   Saul becomes the first king of the Israelites.

928   The Kingdom of Israel splits into Israel (in the north) and Judah (in the south).

722–332   Israel is destroyed by the Assyrians and Judah is overrun by a series of conquerors, including the Babylonians, Persians, and Alexander the Great of Macedon.

142   Jews of Judah revolt against Alexander's successors, the Seleucids.

63   The Romans conquer Judah (which is renamed Judea).

Timeline

928BC
The Kingdom of Israel splits into Israel (in the north) and Judah (in the south)

1882
First Aliyah brings Jewish settlers from Eastern Europe to Palestine

1948
State of Israel declared on May 14; Great Britain withdraws from Palestine

1948–49
First Arab-Israeli War

928BC   1967

AD135
Second Jewish revolt against Romans ends in exile of most Jews from Judea, which is renamed Palestine

1917
Great Britain's Balfour Declaration supports a "Jewish National Home" in Palestine

1947
UN recommends partition of Palestine into separate Jewish and Arab states

1967
Six-Day War

A.D.

135 Second Jewish revolt against Romans ends in exile of most Jews from Judea, which is renamed Palestine.

638 Palestine is conquered by Muslim armies from the Arabian Peninsula.

1517 Turkish Ottoman Empire conquers Palestine.

1882 First Aliyah brings Jewish settlers from Eastern Europe to Palestine.

1897 First Zionist Congress meets in Switzerland.

1917 Great Britain's Balfour Declaration supports a "Jewish National Home" in Palestine.

1920 Great Britain is given a mandate to rule Palestine by the League of Nations.

1939 British white paper severely restricts Jewish immigration to Palestine.

1979
Israel and Egypt sign peace agreement

1995
Prime Minister Yitzhak Rabin is assassinated by an Israeli student

2002
Israel begins constructing controversial security barrier in West Bank

2005
Israel evacuates Gaza Strip settlements and several West Bank settlements

1979 — **2006**

1987
First intifada begins in occupied territories and continues until 1993

2001
Ariel Sharon is elected prime minister of Israel

2004
PLO leader and Palestinian Authority President Yasir Arafat dies

2006
Sharon suffers massive stroke; militant Hamas party wins surprise victory in Palestinian Legislative Council elections

1947	UN recommends partition of Palestine into separate Jewish and Arab states.
1948	State of Israel declared on May 14; Great Britain withdraws from Palestine.
1948–49	First Arab-Israeli War.
1956	Suez-Sinai War.
1967	Six-Day War.
1973	Yom Kippur War.
1977	Likud Party comes to power after two decades of Labor Party rule.
1979	Israel and Egypt sign peace agreement.
1981	Israel annexes the Golan Heights.
1982–85	Lebanon War: Israel attacks Palestine Liberation Organization (PLO) forces based in Lebanon.
1987	First intifada begins in occupied territories and continues until 1993.
1993	Oslo Accords are negotiated by Israel and PLO.
1994	Jordan and Israel sign a treaty of peace.
1995	Prime Minister Yitzhak Rabin is assassinated by an Israeli student.
2000	**July:** Camp David Summit: President Clinton unsuccessfully tries to shape a peace agreement between Israeli Prime Minister Ehud Barak and Palestinian leader Yasir Arafat.
2000	**September:** Second intifada begins.
2001	**February:** Ariel Sharon is elected prime minister of Israel.
2002	**March:** Arab Summit endorses Saudi peace plan: Israel is to give up land it acquired in the 1967 war in return for peace and normalization of relations with the Arab world.
2002	**June:** Israel begins constructing a controversial security barrier in West Bank.
2004	**November:** PLO leader and Palestinian Authority President Yasir Arafat dies.

2005 **August:** Israel evacuates Gaza Strip settlements and several West Bank settlements.

2006 **January:** Sharon suffers massive stroke; the militant Hamas Party wins a surprise victory in Palestinian Legislative Council elections.

2006 **March:** Ehud Olmert is elected prime minister of Israel.

2006 **June–August:** Hizbollah-Israeli conflict in southern Lebanon.

2007 **March:** Arab League renews the Middle East peace offer first made in 2002.

2007 **June:** Hamas fighters stage a violent takeover of the Gaza Strip.

Bibliography

Bard, Mitchell. *Middle East Conflict*. Indianapolis: Alpha Books, 2005.

Bickerton, Ian J., and Carla L. Klausner. *A Concise History of the Arab-Israeli Conflict*. Upper Saddle River, NJ: Prentice Hall, 2004.

Blumberg, Arnold. *The History of Israel*. Westport, Conn.: Greenwood Press, 1998.

Bregman, Ahron. *A History of Israel*. New York: Palgrave Macmillan, 2003.

Congressional Quarterly. *The Middle East*, 11th ed. Washington, D.C.: CQ Press, 2007.

De Lange, Nicholas, ed. *The Illustrated History of the Jewish People*. New York: Harcourt Brace, 1997.

Dickey, Christopher, and Daniel Klaidman. "A Blueprint for Peace." *Newsweek*, April 22, 2002, pp. 28–32.

———. "How Will Israel Survive?" *Newsweek*, April 1, 2002, pp. 22–29.

Gilbert, Martin. *Israel: A History*. New York: William Morrow, 1998.

Humphreys, R. Stephen. *Between Memory and Desire: The Middle East in a Troubled Age*. Berkeley: University of California Press, 2005.

Hirsh, Michael. "The Gaza Effect." *Newsweek*, June 25, 2007, pp. 22–27.

Morris, Benny. *Righteous Victims: A History of the Zionist-Arab Conflict, 1881–2001*. New York: Alfred A. Knopf, 2001.

Perry, Dan, and Alfred Ironside. *Israel at Fifty*. Los Angeles: General Publishing Group, 1998.

Reich, Bernard. *A Brief History of Israel*. New York: Facts on File, 2005.

Sachar, Howard M. *A History of Israel from the Rise of Zionism to Our Time*. New York: Alfred A. Knopf, 2007.

Segev, Tom. *1949: The First Israelis*. New York: Henry Holt and Company, 1998.

———. *One Palestine, Complete: Jews and Arabs under the British Mandate*. New York: Henry Holt, 1999.

Schroeter, Daniel J. *Israel: An Illustrated History.* New York: Oxford University Press, 1998.

Wheatcroft, Geoffrey. *The Controversy of Zion: Jewish Nationalism, the Jewish State, and the Unresolved Jewish Dilemma.* Reading, Mass.: Addison-Wesley, 1996.

Web Sites

BBC: "Israel Today," 1998.

news.bbc.co.uk/hi/english/events/israel_at_50/israel_today

BBC: "Israel and the Palestinians," 2001

news.bbc.co.uk/hi/english/in_depth/middle_east/2001/israel_and_the_palestinians

Britannica Online Encyclopedia 2007, "Israel."

www.britannica.com

Council on Foreign Relations: A Nonpartisan Resource for Information and Analysis: The Middle East

www.cfr.org/region/397/middle_east.html

Council on Foreign Relations: "Terrorism: Q & A/Flashpoint: Israeli-Palestinian," 2002.

www.terrorismanswers.com/policy/israel

Encarta Online Encyclopedia 2007, "Israel."

www.encarta.msn.com

The Jerusalem Post: Internet Edition, 2007.

www.jpost.com

Further Resources

Altman, Linda Jacobs. *The Creation of Israel*. San Diego: Lucent, 1998.

Brackett, Virginia. *Menachem Begin*. Philadelphia: Chelsea House, 2003.

Dubois, Jill, and Mair Rosh. *Israel*. New York: Benchmark Books, 2004.

Greenfield, Howard: *A Promise Fulfilled: Theodor Herzl, Chaim Weizmann, David Ben-Gurion, and the Creation of the State of Israel*. New York: Greenwillow, 2005.

Gross, David C. *Israel: An Illustrated History*. New York: Hippocrene Books, 2000.

Hitzeroth, Deborah. *Golda Meir*. San Diego: Lucent, 1998.

Levin, Aaron. *Testament: At the Creation of the State of Israel*. New York: Artisan, 1998.

Schroeter, Daniel J. *Israel: An Illustrated History*. New York: Oxford University Press, 1998.

Worth, Richard. *Ariel Sharon*. Philadelphia: Chelsea House, 2004.

Web Sites

Council on Foreign Relations: Israel
www.cfr.org/region/406/israel.html

The Israel Ministry of Foreign Affairs
www.mfa.gov.il/mfa

The Israeli Palestinian Conflict in a Nutshell
www.cfr.org/region/397/middle_east.html

The Jerusalem Post: Internet Edition, 2007
www.jpost.com

Picture Credits

Index

About the Contributors

Author **Louise Chipley Slavicek** received her M.A. in history from the University of Connecticut. She has written many articles on historical topics for young people's magazines and is the author of 20 other books for young people, including *Life Among the Puritans*, *Confucianism*, and *Women of the Revolutionary War*.

Series editor **Arthur Goldschmidt Jr.** is a retired Professor of Middle East History at Penn State University. He has a B.A. in economics from Colby College and his M.A. and Ph.D. degrees from Harvard University in history and Middle Eastern Studies. He is the author of *A Concise History of the Middle East*, which has gone through eight editions, and many books, chapters, and articles about Egypt and other Middle Eastern countries. His most recent publication is *A Brief History of Egypt*, published by Facts on File in 2008. He lives in State College, PA, with his wife, Louise. They have two grown sons.